Science Tutor: Physical Science

By

GARY RAHAM

ISBN 10-digit: 1-58037-331-3
13-digit: 978-1-58037-331-9

Printing No. CD-404045

Mark Twain Media, Inc., Publishers
Distributed by Carson-Dellosa Publishing Company, Inc.

Table of Contents

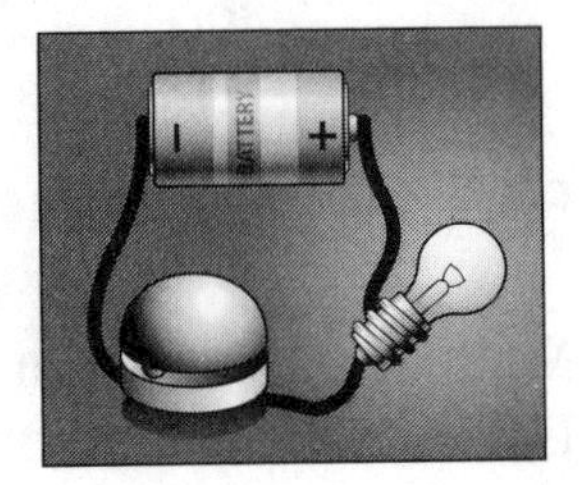

Introduction/How to Use This Book

Physical Science explores the universe of motion, forces, and energy that swirls about us daily but is sometimes taken for granted. Since the metric system is crucial to all scientific measurements, a brief introduction and review is provided in Part 1: Measuring Tools, before launching into the mechanics of motion and forces in Part 2. A metric rule is printed on page 3, but you may want to provide your own rulers and metric measures for some activities. Part 3 examines energy in all its forms, and discusses energy conversions, thermodynamics, energy conservation, and entropy. Buckle-up in Parts 4 and 5 in order to tackle the subjects of electric and magnetic forces and fields and ride the waves of light, sound, and other vibrating disturbances.

All of these topics parallel national science teaching standards for the physical sciences in middle school and above. This worktext will serve as a good review of concepts for some students, an extra opportunity for others to work with difficult concepts again, and can even serve as a teacher's guide for an expanded program of instruction.

Key terms appear **boldfaced** in the text. *Absorb* sections introduce new concepts. *Apply* sections allow the reader to exercise his or her knowledge of the content and concepts by answering questions, filling in the blanks, and engaging in short activities. A few exercises may require additional paper; a calculator may also be useful. At the end of each section, the reader is invited to "put it all together" and test his or her understanding of that section.

Workbooks are never a substitute for hands-on opportunities with simple machines, batteries, circuits, prisms, and magnets. Try to have available as many of these materials as time and budget will allow. If you are a member of the National Science Teachers Association, there is some quite useful software available at www.scilinks.org for creating and tinkering with electric circuits in a "virtual laboratory," where you can explode light bulbs and fry circuits without having to raid the emergency equipment fund.

Enjoy the exciting universe of motion, forces, and energy!

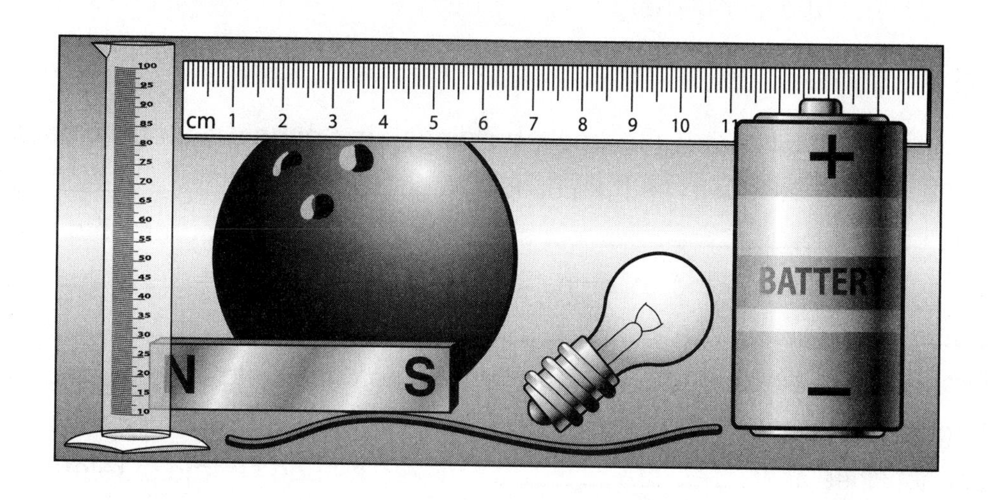

Name: ______________________________ Date: ____________________

A Universe of Motion, Forces, and Energy

A space shuttle can lift a payload equaling the weight of 6.6 tyrannosaurs into Earth's orbit, but to do so, it has to burn 20 times that weight in fuel to counteract the force of Earth's gravity. While you don't have to exert that much energy to hoist yourself out of bed, munch on some Cheerios™, and catch a ride to school, your everyday activities and the launch of a rocket all involve **energy** expended to overcome or generate **forces** that result in **motion**. **Physical science** studies the relationships between motion, forces, energy, and the rules of their interaction.

To discover these rules of interaction, scientists spend a lot of time taking careful measurements. As you may already know, scientists have agreed to use **metric** units of measurements so that scientists all over the world can easily make comparisons. Those 6.6 tyrannosaurs, by the way, weigh 30,000 kilograms (kg), or 10,000 pounds.

When we think about the morning drive to school, we think of the earth as a **stationary**, or non-moving, object. For everyday activities, the earth serves as our **frame of reference** for the motions and forces with which we deal. But we certainly could (and sometimes must) consider other frames of reference in physical science. The earth rotates on its axis at the rate of 1,650 kilometers per hour. Less energy is required to launch a space shuttle in the direction of Earth's rotation than against it, so scientists must expand their frame of reference to include a moving Earth. For launching a shuttle into Earth's orbit, the sun and other planets in the solar system can be considered stationary. Of course, we know that the planets actually move around the sun, so if we planned a journey to Mars, for example, we would have to change our frame of reference yet again. We could consider the distant stars as our stationary frame of reference.

So, fasten your seatbelts and prepare to enjoy the ride as we propel ourselves through a universe of motion, forces, and energy.

APPLY:

1. On a train ride cross-country, the trees, buildings, and people appear to be speeding by the window. This is because the train is our ______________________________.
2. Scientists use the ____________________ system for making measurements.
3. Physical science studies the relationships between ____________________, ____________________, and ____________________.
4. If 6.6 tyrannosaurs weigh 30,000 kg, then what does one weigh? ____________________ Want to give one a lift?
5. For most activities, the ____________________ makes a handy frame of reference.

Part 1: Measuring Tools—Meet the Metric System

Our English system of weights and measures has a colorful history, including a length measurement called the foot based on the shoe size of a king and an inch defined as the length of three barleycorns placed end to end. But English measurements can be confusing and difficult to convert into different units. Scientists use a **metric system** of weights and measures called *Systeme International d'Unites* (SI for short), based on units of ten.

The basic unit of **length** is the meter, which is slightly longer than the English yard. Prefixes are added to indicate measurements that increase or decrease by a factor of ten. So, a **decimeter** is 0.1 m (the prefix *deci* means one-tenth), a **centimeter** is 0.01 m (*centi* means one-hundredth), and a **millimeter** is 0.001 m (*milli* means one-thousandth). To convert from one measurement to another, you simply move a decimal point. If something measures 360 cm, calculate the number of meters by moving the decimal point two places to the left, i.e., 360 cm = 3.60 m.

Going in the other direction, one **dekameter** is 10 m (*deka* means ten), a **hectometer** is 100 meters (*hecto* means one hundred), and a kilometer is 1,000 meters (*kilo* means one thousand), i.e., 1 km = 0.6 miles. The same prefixes are used for all metric units. Other prefixes include *micro* (one-millionth) and *mega* (one million). A **microsecond** is one-millionth of a second, and a **megahertz** is a million hertz (see page 35).

As in English, **seconds** and **hours** are used to measure time. Until 1956, the second was defined in terms of a fraction of the mean solar day, but the day length is slowly increasing as the earth's spin slows. The second is now defined as the time it takes a cesium-133 atom to make 9,192,631,770 vibrations!

The basic metric unit of **volume** is the liter, approximately a quart. A liter is also equal to 100 mm^3 (cubic millimeters). **Area** is measured in square meters (m^2). 1 m^2 is approximately the surface area of a card table. **Mass** is measured in grams and kilograms. 1,000 kg = 1 metric ton, which is nearly the size of an English ton. **Force** is measured in newtons, with 1 newton being about one-fifth of a pound.

The **joule** is the official unit of energy, defined as the amount of work done by a force of one newton acting over a distance of one meter.

Temperature is measured in degrees Celsius (°C), instead of degrees Fahrenheit (°F). The freezing point of water is 0°C and 32°F. **$°C = °F - 32 \times \frac{5}{9}$; $°F = (°C \times \frac{9}{5}) + 32$.**

The theoretical temperature at which atoms can no longer move (will have no more kinetic energy) is called **0 K** (pronounced zero Kelvin). This is also called **absolute zero.** Water boils at 373 Kelvin (the word "degrees" is not used.)

Name: ______________________________ Date: ______________________

Measuring With Metrics

Some common metric conversions are listed below: Refer to this table as necessary when solving problems in this workbook.

1 square meter (m^2) = 10.764 square feet ($ft.^2$)
1 square foot ($ft.^2$) = 0.093 square meters (m^2)
1 square kilometer (km^2) = 0.386 square mile ($mi.^2$)
1 cubic foot ($ft.^3$) = 0.028 cubic meter (m^3)
1 square mile ($mi.^2$) = 2.59 square kilometer (km^2)
1 cubic meter (cm^3) = 35.315 cubic feet ($ft.^3$)
1 cubic inch ($in.^3$) = 16,387.064 cubic millimeters (mm^3)
1 liter (L) = 1.057 quarts (qt.) = 0.264 gallons (gal.)
1 gram (g) = 0.035 ounces (oz.) [avoirdupois]
1 kilogram (kg) = 2.204 pounds (lbs.) [avoirdupois]
1 newton (N) = 0.2248 pounds (lbs.)
1 pound (lb.) = 4.448 newtons (N)

1 meter (m) = 3.28 feet (ft.)
1 millimeter (mm) = 0.039 inch (in.)
1 inch (in.) = 25.4 millimeters (mm)
1 yard (yd.) = 0.914 meters (m)
1 mile (mi.) = 1.609 kilometers (km)
1 kilometer (km) = 0.621 miles (mi.)
1 hectare (ha) = 2.471 acres (ac.)
1 acre (ac.) = 0.405 hectares (ha)
1 quart (qt.) = 0.946 liter (L)
1 ounce (oz.) = 28.35 grams (g)
1 pound (lb.) = 0.454 kilogram (kg)

In addition, 1 L of water weighs 1 kg; 1 mL = 1,000 mm^3 and weighs 1 gram. 1 cubic meter (m^3) of water weighs 1 metric ton. 1 cubic centimeter is about the size of a sugar cube. Sometimes cubic centimeters (cm^3) are referred to as "cc." 1 cm^3 = 1 cc

Directions: Use the metric ruler printed on page 3, the conversion table above, and any other information provided on pages 3 and 4 to help answer the questions below.

1. Measure the length of your index (pointing) finger from its tip to its knuckle joint. Record the length, first in centimeters, then in millimeters. ________ cm ________ mm

   Now, if you ever forget your handy ruler and need to measure something, you can use the finger on your "handy hand" to do so and figure out the actual length later.

2. How tall is this page in index finger units? (You may have to guess a fraction of a finger unit to complete the measurement.) ________ finger units. What is this in centimeters? ________ cm

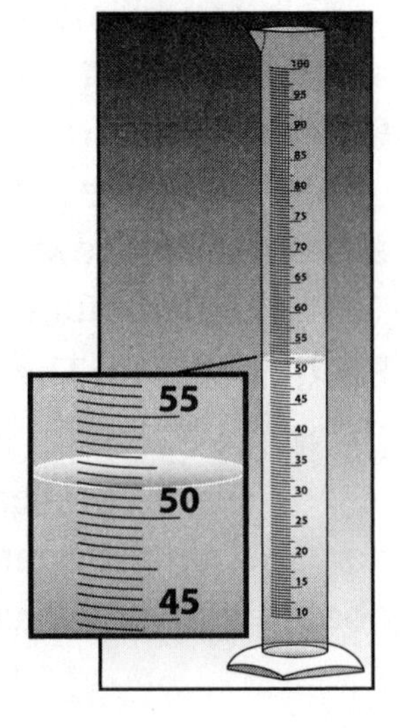

3. The graduated cylinder to the right contains how many milliliters of water? (Each mark represents 0.5 mL.) _______ mL
4. You're fishing at your favorite lake in July. The thermometer says the temperature is 93°F. What is the temperature in degrees Celsius? (to the nearest degree) ________°C
5. How many tons is six megatons? ____________
6. Convert all of the following lengths to millimeters.

   A. 12 cm = ______ mm B. 5 inches = ______ mm
   C. 1 yard = ______ mm D. 1 meter = ______ mm
   E. 10 feet = ______ mm

Part 2: The Mechanics of Motion— Measuring Speed and Velocity

"Move it!" says Dad, and you know you must change your position in a timely manner—which is precisely the definition of **motion**. The **speed** with which you move most likely depends on the loudness of Dad's bark. **Speed equals the distance traveled** (in some metric measure of length, like meters) **divided by the time it takes to move that distance** in seconds or hours: **s = d/t**. By multiplying both sides of this equation by t, you will also see that the distance traveled (d) equals speed (s) times time (t). (**d = st**).

If you want to look cool, you might move at a **constant speed**—that is, you move the same distance during each interval of time measured. If you graph distance moved against time, you get a straight line like the one at the right.

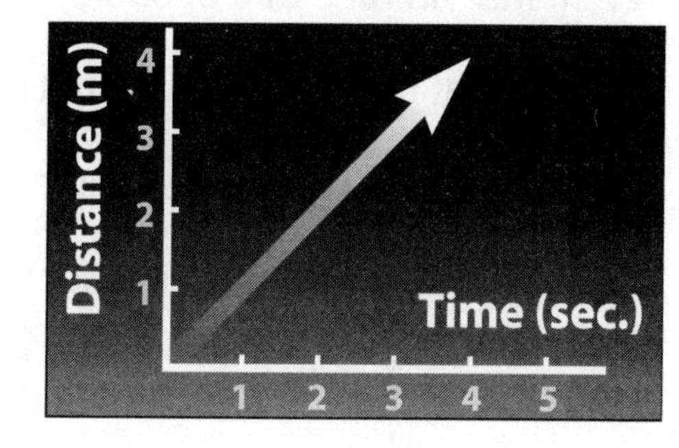

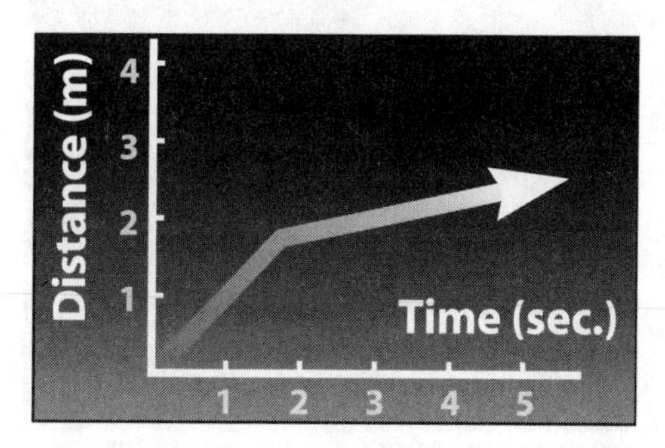

If your coolness takes time to gather, you might move quickly at first, then slow down. A graph might look like the one at the left.

The speed at which you move at any given moment is your **instantaneous speed**. Your **average speed** equals the total distance traveled over the time interval measured. (Average speed and instantaneous speed are the same when speed is constant.)

Velocity is speed in a particular direction. Does Dad want you to come to him or move away? Velocity can be represented by an arrow called a **vector** whose length is determined by the speed moved. These vectors can be added or subtracted. (First you move away from Dad, and then you change your mind and move closer.)

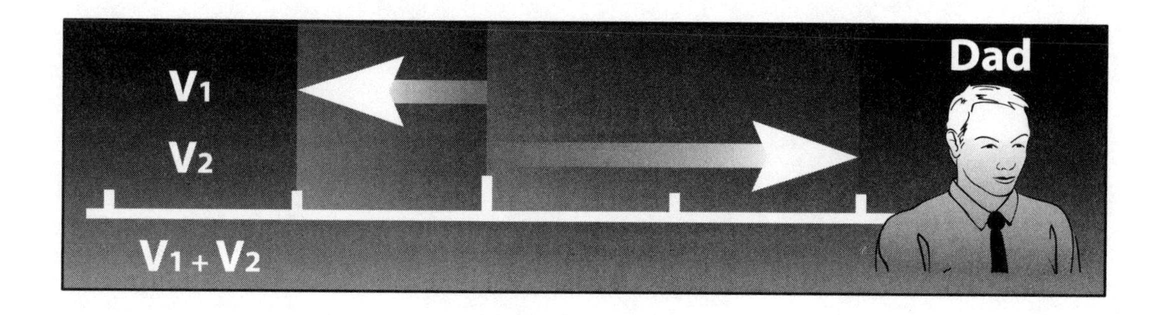

Name: ______________________________ Date: ______________________

Part 2: The Mechanics of Motion: Measuring Speed and Velocity (cont.)

1. What is the speed of a car traveling 144 km in 90 minutes in kilometers per hour?

   ________ km/h In miles per hour? ________ mph

2. If Marvin runs at a speed of 16 km/h, how far will he travel in 45 minutes? ________ km

3. Look at the graph below that measures the speed of a rabbit over the course of an hour.

   What is the rabbit's instantaneous speed at 30 minutes? ________ m/min

   What is its average speed for the entire hour?

   ________ m/min

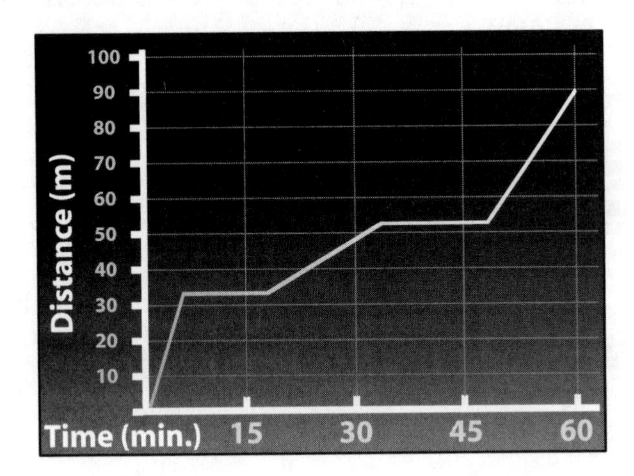

4. Indicate which of the following are speeds and which are velocities:

   A. 125 cm/sec 

   B. 30 km/h northwest ______________

   C. 350 m/sec north ______________

   D. 520 km/h 

5. Let 1 cm = 200 km/h. In the space below, draw a vector that represents the net velocity of a plane that travels 300 km/h north, 175 km/h south, then 225 km/h north.

Name: ______________________________ Date: ____________________

Get Ready, Get Set, Accelerate!

The starter's gun fires. Your thighs tighten as you bolt from the blocks. You go from a standstill (0 velocity) to warp 4 (or so it feels) in just a few seconds. In other words, you have changed velocities, or accelerated. **Acceleration (a) equals final velocity (v_f) minus original velocity (v_o) divided by time (t) elapsed. $a = (v_f - v_o)/t$.** Note that because acceleration involves velocity, it is a **vector**. You don't just speed up, you speed up moving toward the finish line. Note, too, that your body *feels* any change in direction and velocity, whether you are in a race, slamming on the brakes in a car, or screaming as your roller coaster car inverts during the monster loop.

So, let's say you accelerate from 0 m/sec to 3 m/sec in 1 second. Acceleration = (3 m/sec – 0 m/sec)/1 sec or 3 m/sec/sec. In other words, if you maintain that acceleration, your velocity will increase 3 m/sec for every second that passes. At two seconds, velocity would be 6 m/sec, at 3 seconds, velocity equals 9 m/sec, and so forth. Graphs of acceleration are always curved lines.

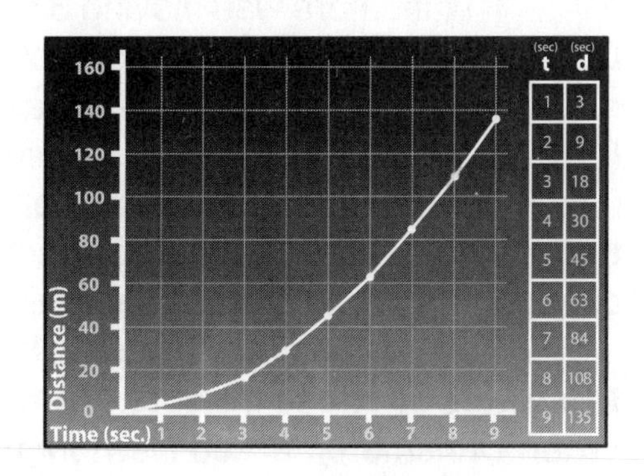

Ichabod was faster out of the blocks, but now his acceleration is decreasing. **Negative acceleration** is commonly called **deceleration**. You leave Ichabod in the dust. The finish line beckons. But then you feel a swoosh of air and smell a hint of perfume. Beatrice passes you. Where the heck did she come from?

Your mom is rotating her arm in a circle, urging you on. Her arm is accelerating, too. *Although the speed of her circles remain the same, the direction of motion of her arm is constantly changing*, meaning the velocity of her arm is changing every moment—the very definition of acceleration.

Can't disappoint Mom. You beat Beatrice by a nose.

APPLY:

1. Using the above graph, how far has the sprinter run after 5 seconds? ________ After 8 seconds? ________. What is her velocity at 5 seconds? ________ At 8 seconds? ________ What is her acceleration between 5 and 8 seconds into the race? ________ (Make sure you give all answers in the proper units.)
2. A car is stopped at a stoplight, but four seconds later is traveling 35 km/h. What is the car's acceleration? ________
3. You are sitting on the couch watching cartoons. Relative to the earth, are you accelerating? ________ Relative to the sun, are you accelerating? ________ Explain your answer.
____
____
4. A runner who pulls a hamstring and has to slow down is:
A. Negatively accelerating. B. Accelerating. C. Decelerating. D. Both A and C.

Name: ______________________________ Date: ____________________

Conserving Mother Mo(mentum)

ABSORB:

136-kg lineman Duane Dunsmore picks up a fumble and heads toward the goal line. He knocks 91-kg Rock Newton on his keister and scores a touchdown. Dunsmore's team, still behind, begins to play harder. The other team begins to make more mistakes. A sportscaster says "Mother Mo has shifted," meaning that the game's momentum has shifted.

Physical scientists define momentum in a specific way: **Momentum equals mass (m) times velocity (v). Momentum = mv**. So, if mass is measured in kilograms and velocity in meters per second, momentum has the units kg-m/sec.

If Dunsmore was moving 3 meters/sec when he hit Newton, what was Dunsmore's momentum? 136 kg x 3 m/sec = 408 kg-m/sec. If Newton was running the same speed, what was his momentum? But what if Newton was running faster? If Newton had been running 5 m/sec, his momentum would have been 455 kg-m/sec, and he could have stopped Dunsmore, even though he was lighter. Bullets have small masses, but they can create great damage because their velocity is so high. Glaciers may creep along at centimeters per year, but their masses are so huge, they can easily plow down entire forests.

For a given set of objects, **the total momentum stays the same unless some outside force acts on those objects. Momentum is conserved** (stays the same) for that set of objects. When Dunsmore decked Newton, the momentum Dunsmore lost was transferred to Newton.

APPLY:

1. What is the momentum of a 0.35-kg blackbird flying at 20 m/sec? __________ (Always give the units in your answer.)
2. Which object has more momentum: a taxi traveling 11 km/h or a baseball pitched at 150 km/h? Explain your answer. ______________________________

   ____
3. What speed would Rock Newton have had to be moving just to counteract the momentum of Duane Dunsmore moving at 3 m per second? __________ m/sec
4. Momentum is the product of an object's ____________________ and ____________________.
5. Katie weighs 68 kg, and Roxanne weighs 45 kg. Both are long jumpers at a track meet. What is Roxanne going to have to do to jump farther than Katie at the meet? ______________

   ____
6. Place the following objects in the correct order from highest to lowest momentum, assuming that they are all moving at their top speed: fly, space shuttle, bullet, Volkswagen, freight train.

   __________ __________ __________ __________ __________
7. When a bowling ball hits the pins at the end of the bowling alley, what happens to the ball's momentum? ______________________________

Name: ______________________ Date: ______________

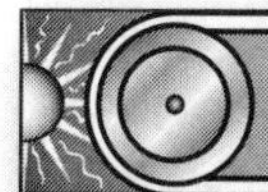

A Feeling for Forces

ABSORB: Your sister falls down. A powerful magnet in a junkyard moves scrap metal. The school bus stops to pick you up. What is responsible for these motions? Forces. Scientifically speaking, **forces are any kind of a push or pull** (including nudges and sucks). Gravity may have caused your sister to fall as it pulled on her unbalanced mass—or you may have pushed her. Magnetic forces pulled on the metal body of an old car. The frictional forces of brake pads touching wheels stopped the motion of the school bus in front of your house. **A force gives energy to an object, either causing it to move, stop, or change direction**.

In the real world, many forces may act on an object at the same time. Gravity tugs at your sister. Wind pushes against her body. But only an **unbalanced force** coming from a **particular direction** will cause her to fall down. Because force acts in a particular direction, it is a **vector** like velocity and acceleration. You can think of forces as arrows whose length indicates magnitude or amount and whose arrowhead points in the direction in which the force is acting. Forces can be added together to get a larger force or subtracted from each other to make a smaller force.

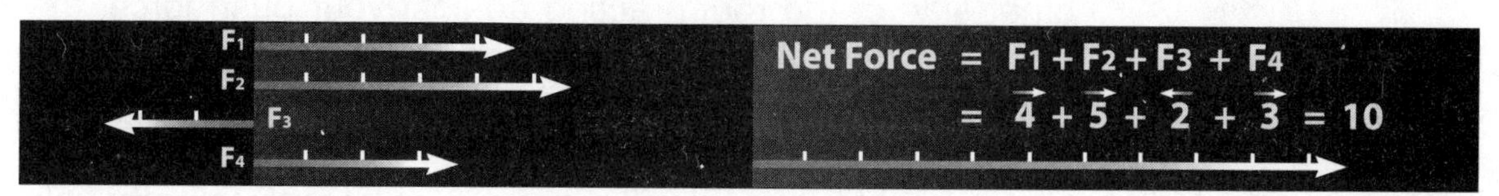

No motion results from the action of **balanced forces**. If you and your brother push equally hard on your sister from opposite directions, she won't move (although she will complain).

We often take **frictional forces** for granted because they are so common. Frictional forces are forces that act in a direction opposite to motion. They are caused by tiny irregularities in solid surfaces that slide past one another as in the case of **sliding** or **rolling friction** (as in brakes and roller skates) and the impact of the molecules of a liquid in the case of **fluid friction**. Fluid friction is usually a smaller force than sliding or rolling friction, which is why the moving parts of engines are greased.

APPLY:

1. Forces are any kind of a ______________ or ______________.
2. T or F? Forces always result in motion.
3. Look at the following force vectors. Measure their length in centimeters, and note their directions. On your own paper, draw one vector that represents all of these forces when they are added together.

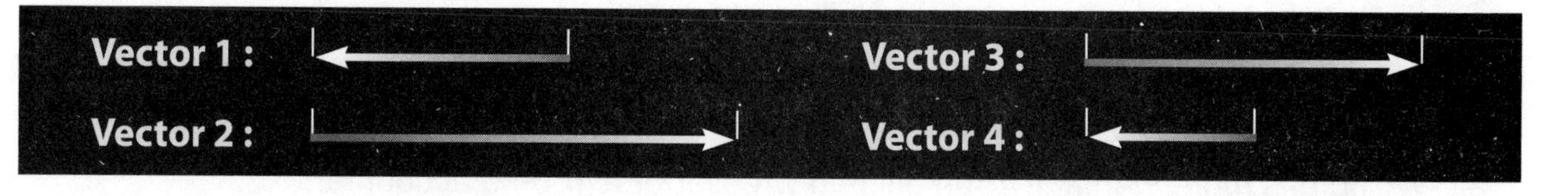

4. Indicate the kind of friction (sliding, rolling, or fluid) represented in the following examples:
   A. A runner sliding into second base: ______________
   B. A girl going down a water-filled slide at an amusement park: ______________
   C. Pedaling a bicycle: ______________

Name: ____________________ Date: ____________________

Newton's Big 3

ABSORB:

"Newton who? Big 3 what?" you might ask. **Sir Isaac Newton** (1642–1727) is considered by some to be the smartest person who ever lived—super nerd #1. Although that opinion can be debated, Newton did discover and invent many things during his lifetime, including **three laws** that summarize the relationship of forces and the motion of objects for all things in the universe (with a few minor modifications under exceptional conditions discovered by Albert Einstein sometime later.)

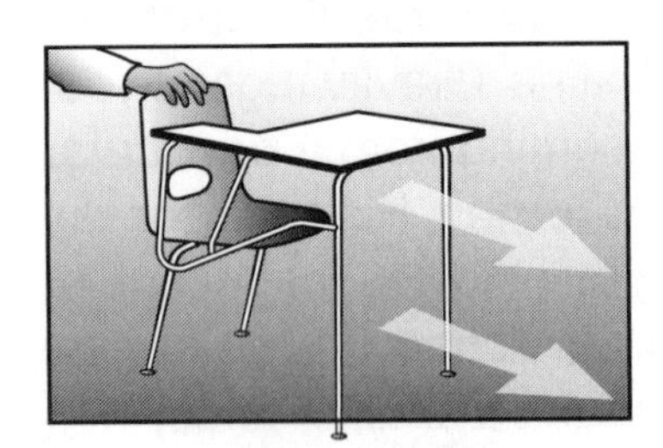

Newton's First Law: An object at rest will stay at rest. An object that is moving will keep moving at a constant velocity unless an unbalanced force acts on it.

Push your empty desk. It moves, then stops. Why? Frictional forces act in the direction opposite to your push. If you put wheels under your desk legs, it moves farther with the same push—less friction. If there were no friction or other forces (like a wall at the other side of the room) acting against your push force, the desk would move forever. This tendency to keep moving is called **inertia** and depends on the mass of the object. A chair will move faster with the same push than the desk. The desk has more mass, and thus more inertia.

Note that the First Law states that an object will move at a **constant velocity** unless an **unbalanced force** acts on it. When an unbalanced force acts to change an object's velocity (direction and/or speed), that object has been **accelerated** (see page 7). This leads to **Newton's Second Law:** The force needed to move an object is equal to the product of that object's mass and acceleration. Written as an equation, it is **F = ma**. The unit of force, honoring Sir Isaac, is called a **newton**. In the metric system, one newton of force is needed to accelerate one kilogram of mass at the rate of one meter per second per second (1N = 1kg-m/sec/sec). If you keep acceleration constant, you can see that it takes more force (and thus more energy) to move the mass of a truck than a motorcycle.

Newton's Third Law: For every action, there is an equal and opposite reaction. Throw a heavy ball away from you, and this law may not be obvious, because you are used to dealing with the force of friction of your feet against the ground. Do the same thing while standing on a skateboard, and you will certainly notice the skateboard moving in the opposite direction from your throw. The same thing will happen if you step too quickly from an unanchored boat to the dock. You could get wet, if you're not careful.

APPLY:

1. What is the force in newtons needed to move a 1,500-kg vehicle at an acceleration of 3 m/sec/sec? ____________
2. Which has more inertia, a 150-kg sumo wrestler or a 100-kg accountant?

   ____
3. How does a bird flying illustrate Newton's Third Law? ______________________________

   ____

Name: ______________________ Date: ______________

Free Fa-a-all and Gravity

Drop a baseball and a bowling ball from the same height, and you will discover they will hit the ground at the same time. Drop them from the roof, and they will not only hit the ground at the same time, but also will be moving faster. All falling objects accelerate at the same rate—a fact not scientifically demonstrated until the late 1500s when Galileo dropped two cannonballs of different sizes from the top of the Leaning Tower of Pisa in Italy.

If an object accelerates, a force must be acting on it. The force acting on falling objects is the force of gravity. Abbreviated "**g**", gravity accelerates falling objects at the rate of **9.8 m/sec/sec**. After one second, an object will be falling at 9.8 m/sec, but after two seconds, it will be falling at the rate of 2 x 9.8 m/sec or 19.6 m/sec. You can do the math. Even a marble becomes a dangerous missile when dropped from a great height.

In the examples above, we have neglected a force that becomes important for light objects (or even fairly heavy objects that have to fall a long way). This is the **upward force of air molecules called air resistance**. When the upward force of air resistance equals the force of gravity, a falling object stops accelerating and reaches a constant **terminal velocity**. The terminal velocity for skydivers is about 190 km/h.

Isaac Newton (remember him?) realized that the force of gravity influenced not only earthly objects, but those in the heavens, too, like the moon. His **Law of Universal Gravitation states that all objects attract each other in proportion to their masses and how far apart they are**. Gravitational force = $\mathbf{G(M_1M_2)/r^2}$, where **G** is a constant (and very small number), $\mathbf{M_1}$ and $\mathbf{M_2}$ are two masses, and **r** is the distance between them.

The **weight** of an object is the force exerted by the force of gravity acting on its **mass**. **Weight = mass x force of gravity**. *An object's mass is always the same* (whether on Earth or in a galaxy far, far away), but an object's weight depends on the large mass it is near.

APPLY:

1. How fast will a mass of water dropped from an airplane be moving after 3 seconds in the air? (Ignore air resistance.) ______________
2. As the distance (r) between two objects increases, what happens to the gravitational force between them? (See the equation for Newton's Law of Universal Gravitation above.) Explain. ______________________________

   ____
3. The planet Mars has a smaller force of gravity than Earth.

   What would happen to your weight there? ______________

   What would happen to your mass there? ______________

Name: ______________________ Date: ______________

Forces in Fluids

ABSORB:

Physical scientists describe **fluids as any material that doesn't maintain a definite shape**. Thus, both liquids and gases are fluids. The molecules that make up these fluids do exert a **pressure** on surfaces with which they come in contact. That pressure (P) equals force (F) divided by area (A): (**P = F/A**). Since forces are measured in newtons and area in centimeters or meters, and area is equal to length times width, pressure units are usually expressed in N/cm^2 or N/m^2. The pressure of air on our bodies at Earth's surface, for example, is 10.13 N/cm^2 at sea level. Lucky for us that our body fluids push back with the same force.

Fluids move from an area of high pressure to one of low pressure. When you suck air out of the top of a straw, you reduce the air pressure at the top of the straw. Normal atmospheric pressure then forces liquid from your drink and up the straw to your lips.

Because gravity pulls on fluids, **pressure in any contained quantity of fluid will increase with depth**. Poke three small holes, one above the other, spaced about 5 cm apart in the side of a plastic milk container. Quickly fill it with water. Water will squirt out farthest from the hole nearest the bottom of the container.

If you jump in a tub of water, you will notice that the water exerts an upward force that keeps you from hitting bottom right away. That **buoyant force is equal to the weight of the fluid displaced by the object**—in this case, your body. This fact, called **Archimedes' Principle**, was discovered by the early Greek thinker, Archimedes, one day in his bath. He was so happy with this insight that he ran naked down the street yelling "Eureka!" An object will float when it displaces a volume of fluid whose weight is greater than or equal to its own weight. Water is unusual in that its density, or mass per volume, is less as a solid than a liquid. Ice floats on water.

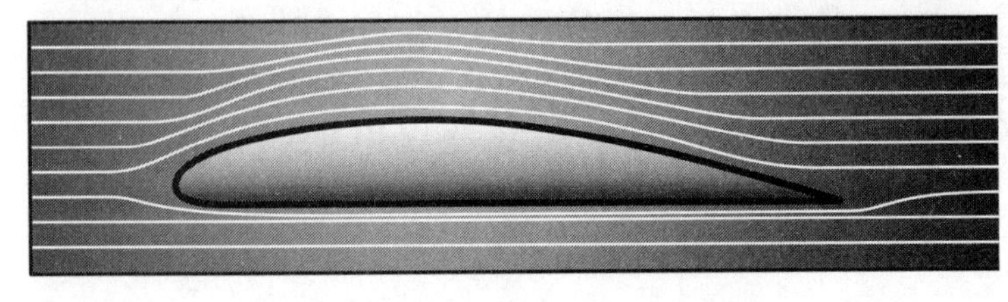

Bernoulli's Principle reveals that the pressure in a moving stream of fluid is less than that in the surrounding fluid. This fact makes flying possible. Stick a scrap of paper in a book and let most of it hang out the side, so it curls toward the ground. Blow over the top of the paper, and the paper will lift as the air pressure above the paper decreases relative to the pressure below. A plane's wings are curved on top and flat on the bottom. Air must travel farther (and faster) over the top surface than the bottom, providing a net upward force beneath the wings. (See the drawing of a plane's wing above.)

APPLY:

1. How is a steel ship able to stay afloat? ______________________________
____
____

2. Why are there winds connecting high- and low-pressure air masses? __________
____
____

Name: ______________________________ Date: ____________________

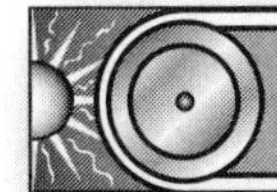

Work and Power

ABSORB:

Pound nails putting up drywall. Lift your baby sister and carry her to the bathroom to change her diaper. Think about how you'll write that English essay. Which of these things is work? "All of it's work," you may want to say, but you sense a trick question. You're right. Work has a specific meaning for physical scientists. **Work, in the scientific sense, only occurs when an object moves in the same direction as the force acting on it**. So, pounding nails is certainly work—as long as the nails move downward when you hit them. Lifting your baby sister is work: you are applying an upward force to lift her. But no work occurs while you are carrying her to the bathroom: you are still applying an upward force to hold her, but the force applied to get her to the bathroom is perpendicular to that force. And, of course, thinking about homework is not work, because nothing gets moved at all.

Work is the product of the force used on an object and the distance it moves. **W = F x d**. Thus, the units of force are the newton-meter, which is given a name all its own: the **joule (J)**. **A force of one newton exerted on an object that moves one meter does one joule of work**.

Power is another term with a specific scientific meaning. Power is a measure of how much work is done within a given length of time. **Power = work/time**, or **power = (force)(distance)/time**. The unit of power, which you can see would be in joules per second, is called a **watt (W)**. **One joule of work done in one second equals one watt of power**. A typical light bulb might have a power rating of 60 W. Electricity is measured in kilowatts (1,000 watts = 1 kW).

APPLY:

1. Work is measured in units called ____________, while power is measured in ____________.
2. Calculate your weight in newtons. (Multiply your weight in pounds by 4.5.) ____________
   If you walked up ten steps that were each 16 cm tall, how many joules of work did you perform? ____________ (In this case, w = weight x height. Remember to convert the distance you moved to meters.)
3. If you walked up the 10 steps in question 2 above in 10 seconds, how much power did you use? ____________. How much power did you use if you ran up the stairs in 4 seconds? ____________
4. Put a check mark next to the activities below that would be considered work under the scientific definition.
   ______ A. Lifting a shovelful of snow
   ______ B. Pushing against a wall
   ______ C. Kicking a soccer ball
   ______ D. Carrying a 50-pound tackling dummy to the locker room
5. How much power in watts is produced by a 1,000 kW generator? ______________ watts
6. T or F? 75 newton-meters is the same as 75 watts of power.

Machines

The robot R2-D2 in *Stars Wars* is a machine, but so are a loading ramp and a crowbar. A **machine** is anything that makes work easier by modifying the work input applied to the machine. A machine can't change the total amount of the input work (which is **effort force x distance**), but it can multiply output force or distance or change the direction in which the force moves. The total amount of work done is conserved. To summarize:

A machine can:

1. Multiply the size of the output force, but decrease the distance over which it acts.
2. Multiply the distance over which the output force moves, but decrease the size of the force.
3. Leave the force and distance of the input work unchanged, but change the direction in which that force moves.

Machines aren't perfect. They lose energy largely through friction. **The efficiency of a machine** is expressed as a **percentage**. (A machine with a two percent friction loss has an efficiency of 98 percent.) The number of times a machine multiplies the effort force is called the **mechanical advantage** of the machine.

Simple machines come in six varieties:

1. The **inclined plane**, which decreases the force needed to lift an object by increasing the distance over which it's lifted, which is why loading ramps are so handy.
2. The **wedge**—actually a kind of mobile inclined plane. Knives and axes are kinds of wedges. The sharper the edge of the wedge, the less effort force is needed to overcome resistance.
3. The **screw** is a kind of inclined plane wrapped around a cylinder. The closer the threads are together, the more the effort force is multiplied (although the distance moved decreases).
4. The **lever** is a rigid bar free to pivot about a fixed point called a **fulcrum**. In a **first-class lever**, the fulcrum lies between the effort force and the resistance. (Think crowbar, seesaw, and pliers.) In a **second-class lever**, the resistance lies between the fulcrum and the effort force. (Think doors, nut crackers, wheelbarrows, and bottle openers.) In a **third-class lever**, the effort force is applied between the resistance and the fulcrum. (Think fishing poles, shovels, hoes, hammers, and baseball bats.)
5. A **pulley** consists of a rope, belt, or chain wrapped around a grooved wheel. Pulleys can change either the direction or the amount of the output force.
6. The **wheel and axle** consists of a large circular object (the wheel) turning about a smaller object (the axle). Force applied to the wheel gets multiplied when transferred to the axle. Screwdrivers, ferris wheels, bicycles, and wrenches are all wheel and axle machines.

A **compound machine** is any combination of simple machines.

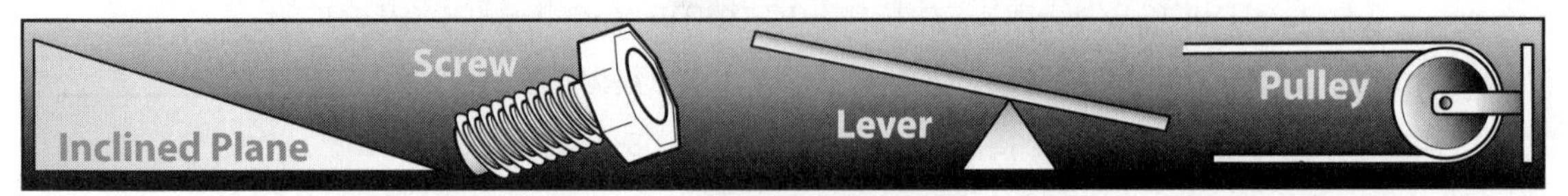

Name: ______________________________ Date: ____________________

Part 2: The Mechanics of Motion: Putting It All Together

CONTENT REVIEW

1. Speed is measured by dividing ______________ traveled by ______________. Velocity is speed in a particular ______________.
2. T or F? Negative acceleration is commonly called deceleration.
3. Explain what it means when a scientist says that "momentum is conserved." ______________
4. Because force, velocity, and acceleration have a particular direction, they are called ______________.
5. Newton's Second Law can be expressed by the formula ______________.
6. If you drop a feather and a cannonball from a height:
   A. They will hit the ground at the same time if no air is present.
   B. The cannonball will hit the ground first in all cases.
   C. The feather is less affected by air resistance.
   D. Both will most likely reach terminal velocity before they hit the ground.
7. ______________ Principle helps to explain how planes can fly.
8. Explain the difference between work and power. ______________
9. Levers, pulleys, and wedges are examples of ______________.

CONCEPT REVIEW

1. Explain what kind of simple machine makes a zipper work. ______________
2. Explain why no work is being done to a bag of groceries while carrying it from the car to the kitchen. ______________
3. If a runner crosses the finish line traveling 16 km/h, what else do you need to know to calculate her acceleration from the start to the finish of the race? ______________
4. If one person runs a race at a constant speed without stopping, but is beaten by another person who stopped several times, what can you say about the second person's *average speed* compared to the first person's *constant speed*? ______________
5. Why must the engine of a large ship be shut off several kilometers before the ship needs to stop? ______________
6. What forces are acting on your body as you sit quietly in a classroom? ______________
7. Name one unbalanced force that might cause you to fall out of your chair. ______________

Name: ______________________________ Date: ____________________

Part 3: All About Energy: Energy, Let Me Count Its Forms

Energy snaps, crackles, and pops all around us. The wind blows, lightning flashes, and living things burn chemical fuels to live and reproduce. For all the things mentioned above and many more, we are dependent on the sun as our source of energy. But exactly what is this stuff?

Energy is the ability to do work. That definition might seem a little vague, except that now you know that work has a precise scientific meaning. Energy represents the ability to exert force and move things in the direction of that force. Like work, energy is measured in joules (which are also newton-meters). Objects can gain energy by work done on them, and energy can convert from one form to another. Let's list the forms in which we encounter energy:

1. **Mechanical energy** is the energy of matter in motion. Moving water and moving air are often used to turn turbines to generate electricity, another form of energy. Race cars, sprinters, and baseballs also possess mechanical energy.
2. **Heat energy** results from the motion of atoms. Slide into home base and your rear end heats up. Friction of one sort or another—the result of matter rubbing against more matter and getting atoms moving—often converts mechanical energy to heat energy.
3. **Chemical energy** is the energy required to bond atoms together. Breaking chemical bonds releases that energy. Your body breaks the chemical bonds in food to provide the energy for carrying out life's tasks.
4. **Electromagnetic energy** is the energy of moving electric charges. The sun's energy reaches us in various forms of electromagnetic energy like visible light, X-rays, and ultraviolet light.
5. **Nuclear energy** is a non-solar form of energy derived from the forces that hold atoms themselves together. When nuclear bonds break (nuclear fission) and atoms decay, nuclear energy is released and converted to heat, which helps warm the earth. (**Geothermal energy** is a byproduct.) When atoms collide under high temperatures and pressures within the sun, they fuse to form different elements and also release vast amounts of nuclear energy.

APPLY:

1. Indicate the kind of energy represented in each example below:
   A. Burning fuel in a car ____________________
   B. Exploding an atomic bomb ____________________
   C. Current moving in a wire ____________________
   D. Tires sliding on pavement when brakes are applied ____________________
   E. Football player running for a touchdown ____________________
2. All forms of energy except nuclear fission come from the ____________________
3. Energy is ____.

Name: ______________________ Date: ______________

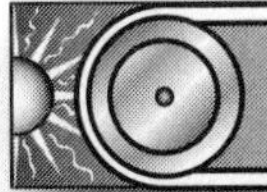

Kinetic Energy: The Energy of Motion

ABSORB:

We defined energy as the *ability* to do work. So, objects can possess energy without actually doing work. We'll discuss that kind of energy—**potential energy**—shortly. When energy does perform work, it is **kinetic energy—the energy of motion**, and all the forms of energy discussed on page 16 can exist as either kinetic or potential energy.

Stretch that rubber band with the spitwad in it. Feel all the potential energy stored there? Your hand may even waver slightly keeping the band stretched. Release the band and most of that potential energy converts to the kinetic energy of the moving spitwad. The precise amount of that kinetic energy is dependent on two factors: the **mass** and **speed** of the moving object. Aha! This sounds very similar to momentum. (Momentum = mv, see page 8.) But momentum and kinetic energy differ in two ways: 1. Momentum is a vector quantity (has direction) and kinetic energy does not. 2. Momentum depends on mass x velocity, but kinetic energy depends on mass x (speed)^2:

K.E. (Kinetic energy) = mass x speed^2/2 or K.E. = mv^2/2

(Note that "v" is commonly used in this equation even though it means speed.) So, let's look at a 45-kg boy walking at a speed of 5 km/h (a 100-pound boy moving at a little over 3 mph). His kinetic energy (ignoring units for the moment) is equal to $(45 \times 5^2)/2 = (45 \times 25)/2 = 562.5$. What happens if you double his mass? K.E. = $(90 \times 25)/2 = 1{,}125$. But, if instead, you take the same 45-kg boy and double his speed K.E. = $(45 \times 10^2)/2 = 2{,}250$. Doubling mass doubles the kinetic energy, but doubling speed increases kinetic energy four times. Because speed is multiplied by itself, this difference increases very quickly. (Triple the speed, and K.E. increases 9 times, but tripling the mass just triples K.E.)

By the way, even though kinetic energy doesn't have direction, just where was that spitwad aimed? Not at the physical science teacher, I hope!

APPLY:

1. Why does it take much longer for a car to stop when applying the brakes at a speed of 60 mph than at 50 mph? ______________________________
____
____
2. Kinetic energy is energy that performs ______________.
3. What is the kinetic energy of a 0.5-kg ball traveling at a speed of 300 m/sec? ____________
4. Explain how momentum and kinetic energy differ. ______________________________
____
5. All forms of energy can exist as either ______________ or ______________ energy.
6. T or F? Energy is the performance of work.

Name: ______________________ Date: ______________

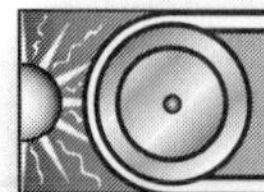

Potential Energy: The Energy of Position

ABSORB:

Potential energy is the energy of position. Think of that stretched rubber band full of energy in your quivering hand. Think of the coiled spring in a jack-in-the-box before someone trips the latch. Think of your big sister, frozen on the couch in front of a video screen. All these things have the capacity or *potential* to do work later with kinetic energy.

Objects with potential energy acquired that energy **when work was performed on them.** You did work to stretch the rubber band. Someone had to push jack into the box and compress his spring. Your sister expended her last shreds of chemical energy to plop her mass on the couch after school.

All forms of energy can exist as potential energy. Both food and organic fuels like gas and oil are potential energy sources until they are burned (combined with oxygen) either through digestion or ignition in a motor. Charge differences between two objects build potential electromagnetic energy until the differences become so great that electrons jump the gap between them, producing a spark. Every atom in and around us carries enormous potential energy that, fortunately, usually requires a great deal of energy to release.

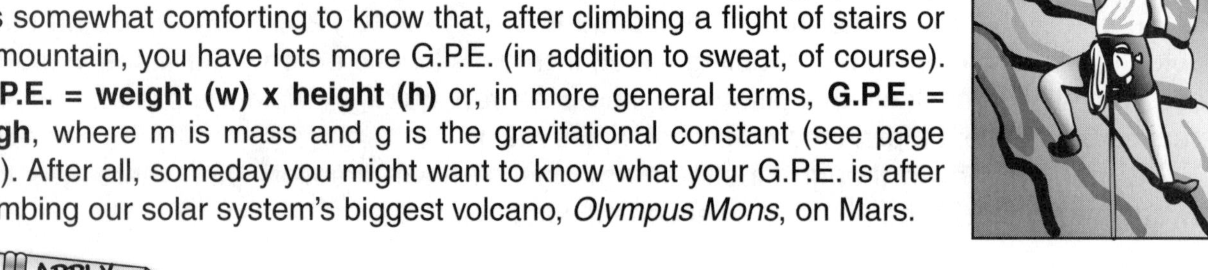

Objects, by virtue of their mass and the pull of gravity on that mass to produce weight, have **gravitational potential energy (G.P.E.)**. It's somewhat comforting to know that, after climbing a flight of stairs or a mountain, you have lots more G.P.E. (in addition to sweat, of course). **G.P.E. = weight (w) x height (h)** or, in more general terms, **G.P.E. = mgh**, where m is mass and g is the gravitational constant (see page 11). After all, someday you might want to know what your G.P.E. is after climbing our solar system's biggest volcano, *Olympus Mons*, on Mars.

APPLY:

1. Potential energy is the energy of ______________.
2. T or F? Potential energy is limited to electromagnetic, mechanical, and nuclear energy.
3. Calculate the G.P.E. in joules of a 675-newton climber at the top of a 3,050-meter mountain in Colorado. ______________ joules
4. Mars has a surface gravity that is only 0.38 (a little over one-third) that of Earth's. Thus, the weight of an object will also be 0.38 times that of Earth. What is the G.P.E. of a climber who weighs 675 newtons on Earth at the top of 26,000-meter *Olympus Mons*? ______________ (I knew you'd want to know this someday!)
5. Objects with potential energy got that energy:
   A. Entirely from their height above the earth.
   B. After work was performed on them.
   C. When kinetic energy was released from fossil fuels.
   D. Through electromagnetic discharges.
6. G.P.E. on Earth is determined by an object's ______________ and ______________.

Name: ______________________________ Date: ____________________

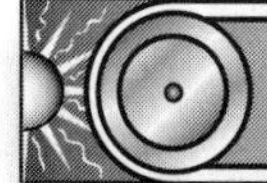

Energy Conversions

ABSORB:

Energy swaps one form for another all of the time. You burn chemical energy in your body to move your finger on a light switch (mechanical energy). The electricity moving in the wiring (electromagnetic energy) changes to light (another form of electromagnetic energy) and some heat energy within a lightbulb filament. Such energy form changes are called **energy conversions**.

Changes from potential to kinetic energy not only occur all of the time, but often occur in a continuous fashion. Remember the last time you swung on a rope? At the beginning and end of the swing you had lots of gravitational potential energy. Your kinetic energy soon increased as your velocity accelerated, reaching a peak at the bottom of your arc. At that point, potential energy briefly reached zero, before increasing again with height. Think about similar changes in kinetic and potential energy in activities like throwing a ball, riding a roller coaster, or falling off a desk. (What were you doing up there anyway?)

All forms of energy can be converted to other forms. Green plants and cyanobacteria routinely convert light energy to the chemical energy of starches and sugars—a good thing for us animals. Sunlight and other forms of electromagnetic energy agitate air molecules, creating heat energy. The stored chemical energy in batteries gets converted to electrical energy to power your iPod™, which gets converted to the mechanical energy of the sound waves of your favorite tunes.

APPLY:

1. When a car engine burns gasoline, ____________ energy gets converted to ____________ energy in the pistons and then to ____________ energy in the turning crankshaft.
2. Changes from one form of energy to another are called ____________________.
3. Assume that your electrical power company gets its energy from a hydroelectric dam. Outline all of the energy changes that occurred from the falling water that turned the generators at the dam to the hot air that was produced from your hair dryer this morning.
   ____
   ____
4. A ball drops from a height, bounces three times, and then rolls to a stop when it reaches the ground the fourth time. At what point is its potential energy greatest? ____________
   At what points does it have zero kinetic energy? ____________________
   When did it have maximum kinetic energy? ____________________
5. A. Give an example of the conversion of light energy to electrical energy.
   ____
   B. Give an example of chemical energy converting to heat energy. ____________
   C. Give an example of mechanical energy converting to heat energy. ____________

Name: ______________________________ Date: ____________________

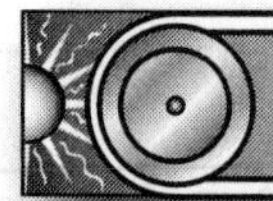

Moving Heat Around: Thermodynamics

The study of heat and its transformation to mechanical energy is called **thermodynamics**. Didn't you always want to be able to use that word during small talk at lunch? Heat always moves from warmer things to cooler things, and it can do so in three ways: **by conduction, convection, and radiation**.

1. **Conduction is heat transfer through direct contact**. Some materials, like metals, conduct heat well because they have some electrons loosely bound to their atoms that are free to bang into other atoms and each other when their energy level is increased. This movement and collision of matter's basic particles creates heat. Contrast good conductors of heat like metals with poor conductors like wool, wood, straw, paper, and styrofoam. These latter materials are also called **insulators**. Fluids (like air) are poor conductors, which is why porous things (containing air pockets) are good insulators.
2. **Convection** is heat transfer through the motion of fluids (like water and air). When a fluid is heated, its atoms or molecules start zipping around, banging into each other and flying apart. Thus, that part of the fluid has fewer particles per area (is less dense) and tends to rise. More dense (cooler) fluid takes its place. This movement sets up convection currents that move heat around. The heat trapped in Earth's atmosphere from sunlight constantly creates convection currents of air that mix warm air from the equator with cooler air near the poles.

3. **Radiation, or electromagnetic waves,** can transmit heat through a vacuum. This **radiant energy** comes in various forms with different wavelengths (distances between wave crests). From longest waves to shortest waves, these are: radio, microwaves, infrared, visible light, ultraviolet light, X-rays, and gamma rays. The shortest waves (having the highest frequency, or rate of vibration) carry the greatest radiant energy. **Radiant energy** of one form or another is generated by all objects. Animal bodies generate considerable infrared radiant energy that our eyes can't see; for example, rattlesnakes possess an infrared sensor that allows them to find prey in the dark. Radioactive substances in the earth, like uranium, emit X-rays and gamma rays when their atoms decay, which keeps the inner earth much warmer than it would be otherwise. Only the sun, however, is hot enough to fuse atoms together and generate radiation at all frequencies.

APPLY:

1. Think about a thermos bottle. It consists of an inner bottle with a shiny silver surface separated from an outer container by a space with no air. In what ways does it block conduction, convection, and radiation? ______________________________

   ____
2. Where and how does most heat loss occur in a thermos bottle? ______________________

   ____

Name: ______________________ Date: ______________

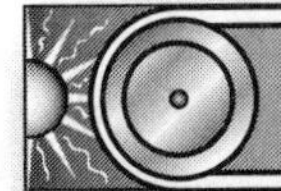

Conserve Energy—That's the Law!

ABSORB:

In the eighteenth century, scientists were learning about many forms of energy, but they were confused about the nature of **heat,** which seemed to be an unwanted byproduct of many energy transformations—usually resulting from the friction between moving parts of machinery. They thought of heat as a weightless substance called **caloric**. Some of the kinetic energy of moving parts always turned into this somewhat mysterious caloric.

Then a man named **James Prescott Joule** (Remember that name?) thought of a clever experiment that showed that the amount of heat generated could be precisely connected to the mechanical energy of motion. He measured the rise in temperature of the water in a beaker caused by the rotation of a paddlewheel turned by a falling weight. He found that the same amount of mechanical energy always produced the same amount of heat. Heat was a form of energy, too! When scientists carefully measured all the forms of energy (including heat) involved in any activity, they found the total amount of energy was always the same before and after, even though energy forms had changed. *They discovered that energy is conserved*—a fundamental scientific concept. This is usually stated as the **Law of Conservation of Energy:** energy can neither be created nor destroyed.

Another scientist with whom most people are familiar, **Albert Einstein**, made a discovery that modified this law in one important way. He found a relationship between mass and energy that is written **energy (e) = mass (m) x c^2** or **($e = mc^2$)**. The "c" is a letter standing for the speed of light, a very large number. Square that number, and you get an even more enormous number. The equation means that a small amount of mass can be—under extraordinary conditions, like at the center of a star—converted to a HUGE amount of energy. (Nuclear bombs later demonstrated that on Earth.) So now the Law of Conservation of Energy is usually stated: energy can neither be created nor destroyed by ordinary means. The total amount of mass *and* energy before and after any event is always the same.

APPLY:

1. T or F? Sometimes energy is lost during a chemical reaction.
2. Newspapers often talk about an energy crisis—about running out of certain energy sources in the not-too-distant future. About which kind of energy sources are they talking?

   ____

   If energy can neither be created nor destroyed, into what kinds of energy have these resources been transformed? ______________________
3. Explain why the phrase "by ordinary means" was added to the Law of Conservation of Energy. ______________________

   ____
4. James Joule showed that ______________ was a form of energy.

Name: ______________________________ Date: ________________

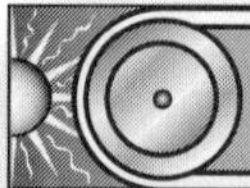

The Laws of Thermodynamics

ABSORB:

Certain laws apply to the way in which heat moves around in the universe. A scientific law, as you saw with Newton's laws, is just a way of summarizing what has been learned about the behavior of matter and energy through long and careful experimentation. We've already discussed conduction, convection, and radiation of thermal energy in terms of the motions of atomic and molecular particles. The **First Law of Thermodynamics** is basically a restatement of the Law of the Conservation of Energy as it applies to thermal energy in more real-world terms: When heat flows to or from a system, the system gains or loses an amount of thermal energy equal to the amount of heat transferred. In other words, you can't get more energy out of something than you put into it. Some of the energy you put in may get some useful work done; the rest generates heat. Push down on the plunger of a bike pump (mechanical energy), and you will move some air into a tire (work accomplished), but you will also notice that the pump gets hot (thermal energy that didn't result in doing work).

The **Second Law of Thermodynamics** says that heat always moves from a hot place to a cold place. The reverse never happens, unless some kind *of work is done on the system in question from the outside*. There's no way your hand will get cold if you touch a hot rock, even if the rock got hotter (which would satisfy the law of conservation of energy). If your girlfriend poured ice water on your hand at the same time, it might get colder, but that would be doing work from outside the hand-rock thermal system.

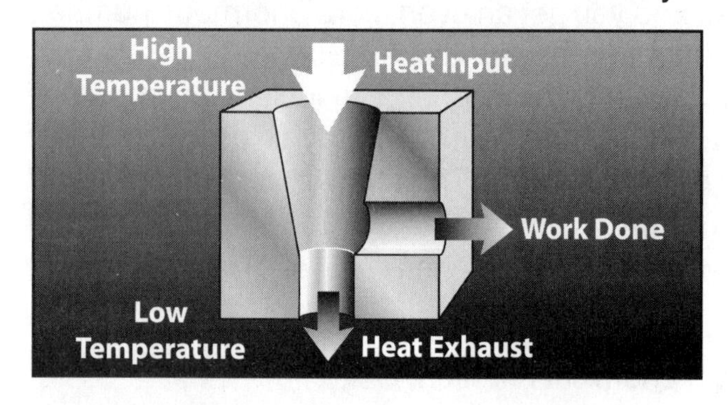

A **heat engine** is any device that changes internal energy into some kind of mechanical work. This includes steam engines, gasoline engines, and most sources of power with which we are familiar. Heat engines can never totally convert heat to work. Something at high temperature (like the burning fuel products in a car engine) heats gases that shove a piston in a cylinder (the work done in an engine), but excess heat is expelled as exhaust. When that excess heat is unwanted, it is referred to as **thermal pollution**, like when a power plant's waste heat warms up a river.

APPLY:

1. If 1,000 J of energy is added to a steam engine, and 400 J of work is done by the engine, how much thermal energy ends up being added to the engine? ________________
2. Which law of thermodynamics relates most directly to the Law of Conservation of Energy?

   ____
3. People once dreamed of creating a perpetual-motion machine—a machine that, once started, would continue to run forever. Why do you suppose such a machine seems to be impossible to build? ____

Name: ______________________ Date: ______________

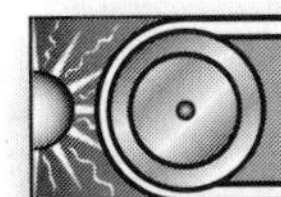
Entropy: A Measure of Disorder

ABSORB:

Very hot things, like the sun, tend to produce more ordered and concentrated forms of energy, like electromagnetic (em) radiation. This energy does work in many ways, including maintaining the activities of all living things. Each time energy is used, however, some portion ends up becoming disordered and diffused thermal energy: heat. Heat is kind of the graveyard of energy transactions. Thus, the **Second Law of Thermodynamics** could be phrased this way: Natural systems tend to proceed toward a state of disorder. Concentrated energy gets used and becomes heat—the last entry in any energy diary.

The **entropy** of a system is a measure of its degree of disorder. The maximum disorder for the universe as a whole will be when everything is the same temperature everywhere—a condition sometimes colorfully called the "heat death of the universe." Fortunately, this can't happen anytime soon. The universe is still cooling down from its fiery beginnings.

Because some of the universe's energy concentrates in hot little packets called stars, the general trend to disorder gets interrupted, most notably in living biospheres like the one that has developed on Earth. Things grow and reproduce, using concentrated energy to do so, but leaving a trail of heat losses behind them. Five billion years or so from now, our sun will go out, eventually followed by all other stars, many of which are yet unborn.

The laws of thermodynamics are sometimes humorously stated this way: You can't win (because you can't get more energy out of a system than you put in); you can't break even (because you can't get as much energy out of a system as you put in); and you can't get out of the game (because the amount of disorder in the universe keeps increasing). Pretty funny, all right!

APPLY:

1. The least usable form of energy is ______________ energy.
2. What kind of music might you expect from a group that called themselves "The Entropics"?
   ____
3. Explain what is meant by the phrase "the heat death of the universe." ______________
   ____
4. Under what circumstances can the general trend to disorder in the universe be reversed?
   ____
5. Name three examples of "concentrated" forms of energy.
   ______________ ______________ ______________
6. The concept of entropy might best be illustrated by:
   A. The birth of a baby.
   B. A construction crew building a skyscraper.
   C. An old building on the verge of collapsing.
   D. The organization of a rock band.

Name: ______________________ Date: ______________

Part 3: All About Energy: Putting It All Together

CONTENT REVIEW

1. Energy is measured in metric units called ______________.
2. An example of electromagnetic energy would be:
   A. A windmill.
   B. A nuclear isotope like uranium.
   C. An X-ray.
   D. Coal.
3. The formula $mv^2/2$ provides a way to calculate the ______________ energy of an object.
4. To calculate the gravitational potential energy of a statue on a 10-meters-tall platform, you would have to know the statue's ______________.
5. When a match is struck, the chemical energy stored in the match's head is converted to ______________ and ______________ energy.
6. Heat can be transferred through ______________, ______________, or ______________.
7. The Law of Conservation of Energy states that ______________________________.
8. "You can't get more energy out of something than you put into it" is basically a statement of ______________________________.
9. T or F? Living things show that the concept of entropy is not true.

CONCEPT REVIEW

1. Explain why mines dug deep within the earth are often quite hot. ______________________________
2. What kind of energy does not do work? (and don't say the lazy kind!) ______________________________
3. Sir Marvin decided to improve the destructive power of his cannon by increasing the size of his cannonballs. Sir Seymour kept his cannonballs the same size, but improved his powder to provide more velocity. Which knight will have the more destructive cannon? ______________ Why? ______________________________
4. Jupiter is a more massive planet than either Saturn or Earth. Saturn is more massive than Earth. On which planet would an astronaut weigh the most? ______________
5. T or F? Radiant energy is generated by a petunia on Tuesday.
6. In terms of the laws of thermodynamics, explain why a refrigerator vents hot air. ______________________________

Name: ______________________________ Date: ______________

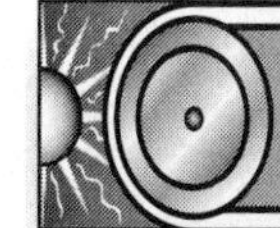

Part 4: Electricity and Magnetism: Force, Charge, and Atomic Structure

We've learned a little bit about how masses attract each other with gravitational forces, but there are other attractive forces in the universe that are much stronger: the force between **electrically charged particles**. Such particles may also repel each other. The nature of these forces has to do with the way in which matter is put together with tiny particles called **atoms**.

Three particles—**protons**, **neutrons**, and **electrons**—come together to create an atom. Electrons, which are very tiny, carry a **negative charge**. Protons are 1,800 times bigger than electrons, but they carry an equal, but opposite, **positive charge**. Neutrons, just slightly bigger than protons, are electrically neutral. Protons and neutrons contain most of the mass of an atom and form its center, or **nucleus**. Electrons orbit the nucleus in a kind of cloud of negative charge. Most matter contains an equal number of protons and electrons, making it electrically neutral, but electrons can be stripped from one atom and added to another. When this happens, the atom losing one or more electrons has a net positive charge, and the one gaining one or more electrons becomes negative. **Like charges repel each other. Unlike charges attract**.

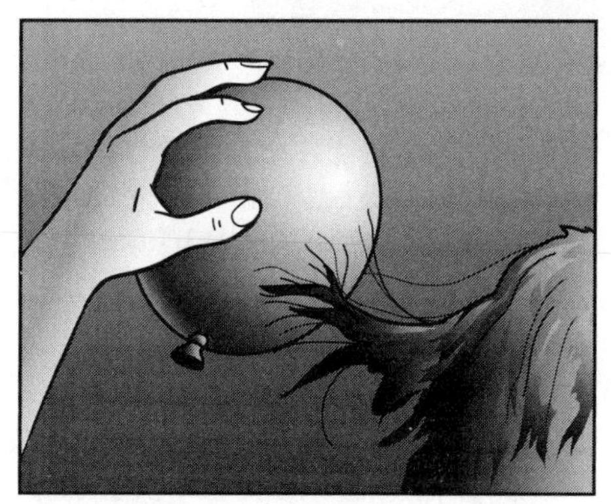

If you rub a balloon on your hair, the balloon will remove some electrons. The balloon becomes negative, and your hair becomes positive. Hold the balloon a short distance from your hair (without touching it) and you have a bad hair day, as strands of hair reach for the balloon. The unit of charge is called a **coulomb** and represents about 6.28 billion billion electrons. That's a bunch, sure, but it is only about the amount of charge that passes through a 100-watt light bulb in one second.

Rub the balloon on your hair again, then stick it to a wall. The wall should be electrically neutral. Why the attraction? The negative charge of the extra electrons on the balloon are pushing away the electron clouds of the wall's atoms, separating the positive charge of their nuclei and the negative charge of the surrounding electron clouds. The balloon is attracted to the positive nuclei, which are now slightly closer to it. This process is called **inducing an electric charge** in a substance.

Rub that balloon on your hair again. (Hope you're not getting a bald spot!) Now place an empty aluminum soda can on its side on a smooth surface. Place the balloon near the side of the can at a low angle. You should be able to push it along without touching it. You can induce an electrical charge in metals easily because they have loose outer electrons free to roam throughout the metal.

APPLY:

1. What is the charge of an atom with 20 protons and 18 electrons? ______________
2. Water molecules are positive on one end, negative on the other. Predict what a negatively charged balloon will do when placed close to a stream of water. ______________

   ____

Name: ______________________ Date: ______________

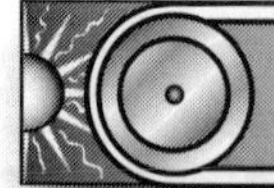

Electric Forces and Fields

By pushing a soda can around with electric charge, you've shown that an **electrical force**, like a gravitational one, can act between objects that are not in direct contact. In fact, the strength of that force, described by **Coulomb's Law**, looks a lot like Newton's gravitational force (see page 11): $\mathbf{F = kq_1q_2/d^2}$ (q_1 and q_2 are electrical charges, k is a constant, d is the distance between the charges). However, k in this case is a much larger number.

The space between two charged objects through which electrical force acts is called an **electric field**. An electric field has both **strength and direction;** therefore, it is a vector quantity, like velocity and acceleration. **An electric field travels away from a positive charge and toward a negative one**. The electric field between two charged particles would look like this:

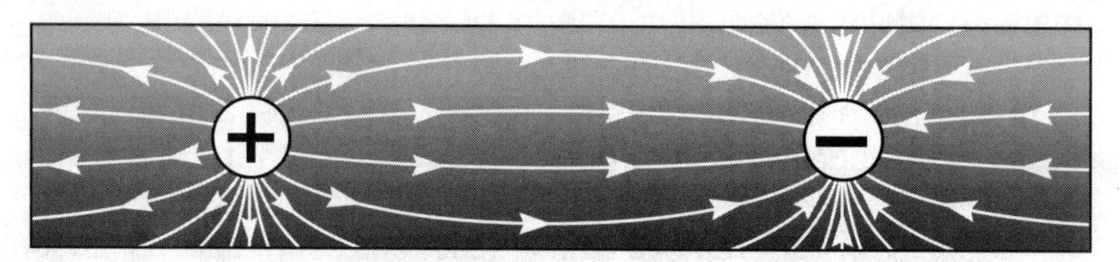

A charged particle placed in an electric field will feel a force in the direction of the electric field.

Just like a rock on a shelf has gravitational potential energy, a charged particle just sitting around has **electrical potential energy**—it has the capacity to do work, although it isn't doing it at the moment. Work is required to move a charged particle against the electric field of another charged particle. It's convenient when speaking about electric charges to think about the amount of electrical potential energy per unit of charge, which is called **electric potential**. Electric potential = electrical potential energy/amount of charge. Electric potentials are measured in **volts**. One volt is the electric potential of one joule of energy per coulomb of charge. **1 v = 1 J/1C**. Electric potential is often just called **voltage**.

When two ends of a metal wire have an electric potential difference between them, this voltage difference acts like a kind of "electric pressure" that causes electrons to move. Moving electrons are the same as an **electric current**.

APPLY:

1. T or F? An electric field has strength, but no direction.
2. T or F? The force of attraction between a positive and negative electric charge decreases quickly as the distance between them increases.
3. Explain the difference between electric potential and electrical potential energy.

   ____

4. An electric field travels (toward or away from) ______________ a negative charge.
5. An electric current will flow when there is a ______________ difference between two ends of a metal object.

Name: ______________________________ Date: ______________________

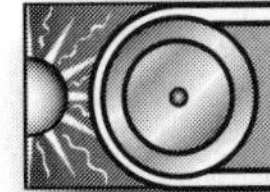

Magnets and Magnetic Induction

Now that you're all warmed up thinking about electric charges and currents, we're going to talk about **magnets** and **magnetism**. "Why?" you might reasonably ask. There is a connection—a very close one, in fact—which we will discuss in just a couple of pages. Trust me.

Most people are at least somewhat familiar with magnets. Your mother probably has your picture stuck on the refrigerator with one. They come in motors and other electrical equipment, and you're not supposed to get them near computers. Magnets attract or repel other magnets with something called **magnetic force**. They also exert an attractive force on some, but not all, metals. Magnets have two poles, a north one and a south one—like the earth.

If you have access to two bar magnets, hang one from its center so it is free to rotate. If you bring the north pole of the second magnet near the south pole of the first, they will attract each other. If you bring the north pole of the second magnet near the north pole of the hanging magnet, a force will push them apart, making the hanging magnet rotate. **Unlike poles attract, and like poles repel**. This is exactly the same way in which electrical charges work.

But magnetic poles are different from electrical charges in one important way: You can't have a magnetic pole that exists all by itself—a **monopole**. There is no magnetic equivalent to positively charged protons and negatively charged electrons. If you cut magnets in half, they still end up with north and south poles.

However, just as with electric induction, magnets can *induce magnetism* in those materials they attract, like iron. Pick up a paper clip with a strong magnet, and you can use that paper clip to pick up other ones. It has become a victim of **magnetic induction**.

As you know, the earth has a magnetic field, although what is called the north pole of Earth is really its southern pole, magnetically speaking. A compass is a device with a magnetized needle whose magnetic north end is free to swing and point toward Earth's magnetic south pole (which is called the north pole). Dizzy yet? Also, Earth's magnetic poles wander a bit and don't exactly coincide with the geographical North and South Poles.

APPLY:

1. Circle the letter of the best answer.

   Magnetic poles and electric charges:

   A. Attract and repel each other in similar ways.

   B. Are alike in all ways.

   C. Can both induce magnetism in iron.

   D. Can both induce electric charge in metals.

2. The north pole of magnet A will ______________________ the south pole of magnet B.
3. Magnetic ______________________ don't exist.

Name: ________________________________ Date: ____________________

Magnetic Fields

ABSORB:

Since magnets exert forces on each other without direct contact, magnets, like electrical charges, generate a force field in the space around them called a **magnetic field**. This is most easily seen by sprinkling iron filings on a piece of paper lying directly over a magnet. The filings will line up along the magnetic field lines. **The field is strongest** where the lines are closest together at the poles. Magnets with field lines close together are stronger than magnets with field lines farther apart. If you move a compass around a bar magnet, you will see that the needle (a small magnet, itself) **points in the direction of the field lines, which are from north pole to south pole**.

Why do some materials—notably iron, but also nickel and cobalt—respond so readily to magnetic fields? The short answer is that these materials are made up of atoms that act like minute magnets themselves. These atoms line up along magnetic field lines in clusters of billions of atoms called **magnetic domains**. Domains line up in super clusters of domains as well. When this happens, iron and other **ferromagnetic substances** become magnetic in the process of magnetic induction discussed on page 27. When not induced to line up by magnetic lines of force, domains tend to reorient in random fashion through the normal movement of atoms in response to heat. In this condition, they are not magnetic.

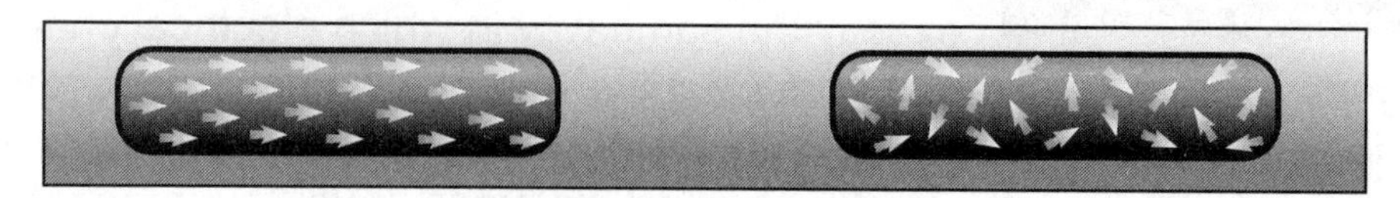

By looking at the figure above, it's easy to see why cutting magnets into small pieces just results in making smaller and smaller two-pole magnets and not monopoles (see page 27).

APPLY:

1. Magnets produce ______________________ in the spaces surrounding them.
2. If magnets are knocked around a lot or heated, their magnetism will be reduced or lost. Explain why. ____

   ____
3. Give three examples of ferromagnetic metals: ______________, ______________, ______________
4. Magnetic field lines begin at the ______________ pole of a magnet and end at the ______________ pole.
5. In the picture below, which is the stronger magnet? ____________
6. Magnetic domains are clusters of billions of ____________ aligned along the direction of magnetic ____________ ____________.

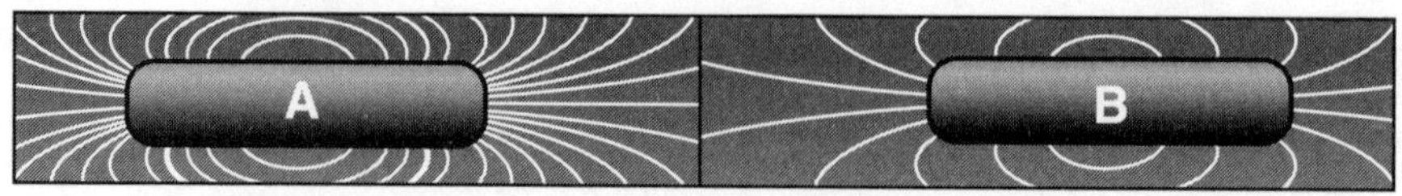

Name: ______________________ Date: ______________

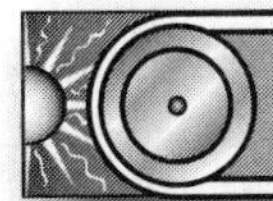

Forces, Electric Currents, and Magnetic Fields

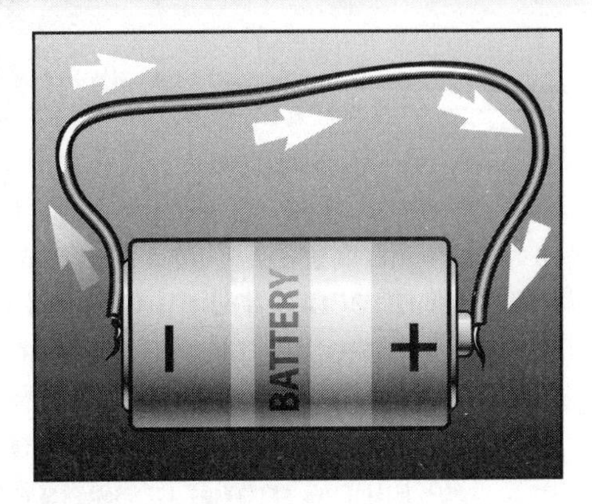

At the end of page 26, we described an **electric current** as the movement of electrons. One easy way in which to generate an electric current is to connect a wire to the two terminals of a battery. Chemical energy in the battery generates excess electrons at the negative terminal that flow through the wire to the positive terminal.

In 1820, the scientist **Hans Christian Oersted** made a fundamental discovery: an **electric current generates a magnetic field**. It's easy to demonstrate not only that this happens, but what the field looks like: hold a compass over a wire in which a current is flowing. The compass needle will swing to point at **right angles to the wire**. Hold the compass below the wire, and the needle will swing completely around to point in the opposite direction (but still at right angles to the wire). The current in a wire generates a circular magnetic field around itself. (If you curl the fingers of your left hand around a wire and extend your thumb, your thumb points in the direction the current is moving, and your fingers curl in the direction of the magnetic field.) When the current does not flow, the magnetic field disappears. Electricity and magnetism are two aspects of the same **electromagnetic force**.

This helps to explain the nature of magnetic domains. Because atoms contain outer regions of moving electrons, and because moving electrons are essentially electric currents, atoms also generate magnetic fields. In most atoms, these magnetic fields tend to cancel each other out, but the atoms of ferromagnetic substances, like iron, possess excess magnetism. They possess large **magnetic moments**.

If you place two wires with current flowing through them close together, they will either push each other apart or attract each other, depending on whether currents are moving in the same or opposite directions, because the associated magnetic fields will also be either aligned or opposite. A coil of wire with current flowing acts just like a permanent magnet with north and south poles. Current flowing through wire wrapped around an iron nail will induce the nail's magnetic domains to line up, producing an **electromagnet**.

APPLY:

1. Hans Christian Oersted discovered that:
   A. Atoms possess magnetic moments.
   B. Electromagnets are easy to make.
   C. Electric currents produce magnetic fields.
   D. Electric currents consist of moving electrons.
2. T or F? A magnetic field continues to exist around a wire that is no longer carrying an electric current.
3. Iron atoms possess large ______________ ______________.

Name: ____________________ Date: ____________________

Linking Moving Charges and Changing Magnetic Fields

Electric currents produce magnetic fields. Magnets, in turn, can influence the flow of electric currents. If you move a wire through a magnetic field, a current will flow in that wire. This is the basis of electric **meters** and **motors**.

A compass represents a simple meter to measure whether or not a current is flowing in a wire. If you place a compass needle in the middle of a coil of wire, the needle will move and record the magnetic fields produced by even small currents of electricity. This latter device is called a **galvanometer**. A galvanometer can be calibrated to measure the rate of the current flow in amps, in which case it is an **ammeter**. A **voltmeter** is a kind of galvanometer calibrated to measure electric potential in volts.

A simple **motor** consists of a loop of wire (**armature**) suspended between the poles of a magnet. The wire ends connect to a metal loop called a **commutator** separated into two halves, one-half connected to the positive terminal of a battery and the other to the negative terminal. Current flows from the negative terminal through the loop, generating a magnetic field that forces the loop to turn against the field of the motor magnet. The turning loop would be forced backward after a half-turn as it began to cut the magnetic lines of force in the opposite direction, except that the gap in the commutator reverses the direction of flow of the current generated by the battery in the loop. This keeps the loop spinning in the same direction so that it can turn a shaft of some kind to rotate the wheels on a Ferrari or run an electric cake mixer.

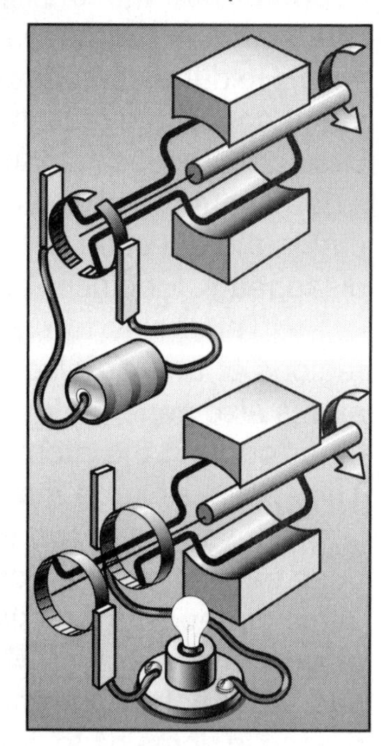

To create a simple **generator** of electric power, you must reverse the process. Water, for example, can provide the mechanical energy to rotate loops of wire in a magnetic field. The magnetic field generates current in the wire to run electric devices. Because the voltage varies or alternates in a regular fashion as the loop turns, this is an **alternating current**, or **AC** generator. AC current is standardized so that the current goes through 60 cycles of change each second (60 Hertz).

APPLY:

1. A(n) ____________________ is generated in a wire when it moves across a magnetic field.
2. Ammeters and voltmeters are different kinds of ____________________.
3. The purpose of a commutator in a motor is to ____________________

   ____
4. T or F? The purpose of a generator is to convert electrical energy into mechanical energy.
5. Why does a compass give unreliable readings when used near electrical appliances?

   ____

EMFs and Circuits

The chemical energy of batteries converts to electrical energy when the potential energy of charge differences between two terminals is allowed to "fall" and become the kinetic energy of moving charges. This charge difference in a battery is called the **potential difference** and is measured in **volts**. Anything like a battery that moves charges across a potential difference is called an **electromotive force**, or **emf** for short.

You can give electrons something to do by connecting a wire to the terminals of a battery and letting them run from negative to positive terminal. This creates a **circuit**, or closed pathway, for electron travel. Normally, however, we want electrons to do some useful work along the way like running a can opener or DVD player.

So, for an electric current to do work, you need:

1. An emf (battery or other electromotive force);
2. A complete circuit connecting the terminals of the emf; and
3. A device connected so that it is part of the circuit.

Note: Although we know that electrons, which are negatively charged, do the moving in a circuit, by convention the flow of electric charge is considered to be a movement of positive charge. This doesn't affect the logic of how circuits work, but may be confusing when current flow is discussed.

If you connect objects (like light bulbs) in one continuous string so that current must flow through each object to complete a circuit, you have created a **series circuit**. If, however, you create a separate path for each object in the circuit and then bring the paths back together before reaching the second terminal, you have created a **parallel circuit**.

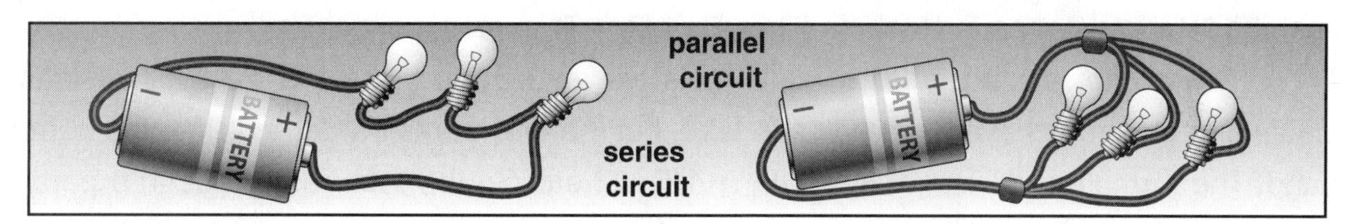

Shortly we'll see how objects behave differently in series and parallel circuits.

1. Does a 1.5-volt battery or a 12-volt battery have a higher potential difference?

 ____

2. Both a car battery and an AAA battery are examples of ________________ forces.
3. Besides having an emf, what is necessary for an electric current to perform useful work?

 ____

 ____

4. Electric current is considered the movement of ________________ charges, even though we know current is the movement of electrons.
5. On your own paper, diagram a series circuit containing a battery, a light bulb, and a bell.

Name: ______________________ Date: ______________

Ohm's Law and Resistance

As you know from Part 3 of this book, any energy conversion results in heat losses—nature's tax on energy transactions. In the case of emfs and electric circuits, most of that heat results from electrons banging into all those subatomic particles on the way to the next electrode. How much a wire, a light bulb, or any other device resists the flow of electrons is called **electrical resistance**. Resistance is measured in units called **ohms**, named after George Ohm, a physicist who discovered a very important relationship between voltage, current, and resistance.

All objects in a circuit resist electron flow, but copper wires have so little resistance that it is usually ignored in calculations. The relationship uncovered by Ohm is simply that the voltage across a device is equal to the product of the current through the device and the resistance of the device to current flow. As an equation:

V (in volts) = I (in amps) x R (in ohms) or V = IR

So, if you have a current of 1.2 amps flowing through a device with a resistance of 10 ohms, the potential difference is 12 v. This relationship is called **Ohm's Law**. Using a little algebra, this formula can be re-arranged to solve for current or resistance. **I = V/R**, for example. What does R equal?

Sometimes you may want to slow the flow of current in a circuit—if you have a device that can't handle a lot of current. In such cases, you can add a **resistor** to a circuit, which is a device that does nothing but slow electrons down. Remember, though, that every device in a circuit is a kind of resistor.

In a **series circuit**, the total resistance is just the simple sum of all the individual **resistances**. So if a light bulb has a resistance of 5 ohms and a bell has a resistance of 10 ohms, the total resistance is 15 ohms ($\mathbf{R_T = R_1 + R_2 + R_3}$....etc.)

In a **parallel circuit**, adding more resistors actually reduces the overall resistance, because the electrons have more paths to take, but the emf works harder to pump the current around. The formula is $\mathbf{1/R_T = 1/R_1 + 1/R_2 + 1/R_3}$ ..., etc. So the total resistance in a parallel circuit containing the same light and bell would be $1/R_T = \frac{1}{5} + \frac{1}{10} = \frac{2}{10} + \frac{1}{10} = \frac{3}{10}$. So $R_T = 3.33$ ohms.

APPLY:

1. Electrical resistance is a measure of resistance to the flow of ______________.
2. T or F? Adding an extra object to a series circuit will decrease the overall resistance in the circuit.
3. What is the current flow in amps in a circuit with an emf of 20 v and a total resistance of 4 ohms? ______________
4. What is the resistance in a circuit with a 1.5-v battery and 10 amps of current? ______________

Name: ______________________________ Date: ______________

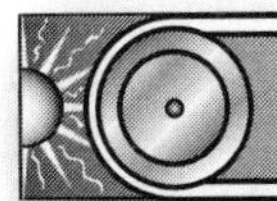

Power Production and Transformers

ABSORB:

Nikola Tesla and **George Westinghouse** collaborated to find a practical way of changing lots of mechanical energy (the falling water of Niagara Falls) into easily transportable electrical energy. Tesla designed armatures for generators (see page 30) that consisted of tightly wound coils of wire that could be spun quickly in magnetic fields by water or steam-driven turbines. The resulting alternating current induced in the wire could be sent safely over long distances with the help of **transformers** to alter voltage as necessary.

A transformer consists of two coils of wire, a **primary input coil** and a **secondary output coil,** usually wrapped on the same iron core. When a current flows in the primary coil, it produces a magnetic field. When that magnetic field intersects the second coil, it induces a voltage in it. If the primary and secondary coils are equal in size, the voltage induced in the output coil equals the voltage of the input coil. But if the secondary coil has more turns, the voltage induced there will be larger. This is called a **step-up transformer**. If the secondary coil has fewer turns, it produces less voltage and is a **step-down transformer**.

Primary voltage/# turns of wire in primary coil = Secondary voltage/# turns of wire in secondary coil.

Step-up transformers don't provide something for nothing. (Remember the Law of Conservation of Energy.) The higher voltage produced comes with a smaller current. But it's safer and easier to transport electricity at high voltage and low amperage, then step down voltage (and increased amperage) at the user end. Recall that the rate of transferring energy is power. **Power = Voltage (V) x Current (I)**. Power into primary = power out of secondary (less heat losses, of course). So, $\mathbf{(VI)_{primary} = (VI)_{secondary}}$

APPLY:

1. T or F? A transformer is a device that can only increase the voltage carried in power lines.
2. Describe the difference between a step-up and step-down transformer.

 ____

 ____

 ____

3. The primary coil in a transformer has 250 turns; the secondary coil has 500. It is safe to say that:
 A. This is a step-down transformer.
 B. The voltage in the secondary coil will be higher than in the primary.
 C. The power in the secondary coil is greater.
 D. The power in the primary coil is greater.
4. Electrical energy is often transformed from the ______________ energy of falling water.
5. T or F? Transformers violate the Law of Conservation of Energy.

Name: ______________________ Date: ______________

Part 4: Electricity and Magnetism: Putting It All Together

CONTENT REVIEW

1. Indicate the charge carried by the following atomic particles:
   Proton: __________ Neutron: __________ Electron: __________
2. An electric field travels away from a ______________ charge and toward a ______________ charge.
3. T or F? Like poles of a magnet attract each other, and unlike poles repel each other.
4. What is a magnetic domain? ____
5. T or F? A permanent magnet and a coil of wire carrying a current both produce magnetic fields.
6. If you move a wire through a magnetic field, a __________ will flow through the wire.
7. An electric current can perform work as long as there is a battery to produce current, some device to operate, and everything is connected in a complete ______________.
8. What is the formula for Ohm's Law? ______________ What units are used to express current? ________ What units are used to express potential difference? ________
9. What do you know about the number of turns of wire in the secondary coil of a step-down transformer compared to the number of turns in its primary coil? ______________

CONCEPT REVIEW

1. Coulomb's Law states that the force between two charged particles equals kq_1q_2/d^2. How is this relationship similar to the gravitational force between two objects, and how is it different? ______________
2. There are some very small pieces of hair in a bottle of baby oil. Marvin rubbed a balloon on his sweater, then put the balloon near the bottle. The hairs in the bottle all lined up pointing toward the balloon. Explain what is happening. ______________
3. Bridget tried to play with her magnet while taking a steaming hot bath, but it didn't work very well. Why? ______________
4. Osgood connected a loop of wire to the terminals of a toy railroad transformer. At one point in the loop, the wires came very close together. When Osgood turned on the power, the wires seemed to push apart where they were closest. Explain. ______________
5. A circuit has three lights. Jezebel removed one light from the circuit, and the other two glowed more brightly. Were the lights connected in series or parallel? Explain. ______________

Name: ______________________ Date: ______________

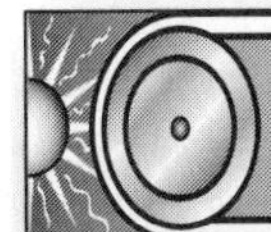

Part 5: Waves of Light and Sound: Waves and Their Properties

Skip a stone on quiet water, and water waves will fan out from every spot the stone hits. Some of the mechanical energy of your throw has created a disturbance in the water that carries away mechanical energy of its own in the form of **waves**. Waves result from vibrations, and **vibrations** are the repeating motion of things along the same path.

Waves in water are an example of **mechanical waves**—waves that require some sort of **solid, liquid, or gaseous medium** through which to pass. The energy of the rock hitting water forced water molecules to move quickly away in all directions. Those molecules hit other molecules, which then hit additional molecules in an expanding and repeating pattern. Sound is a mechanical wave transmitted through air and, with more difficulty, through liquids and solids. Earthquakes result from waves transmitted through solid ground.

Electromagnetic waves, like light, depend on the vibration of electric and magnetic fields to carry energy, and they require no medium. They can pass from the sun or other source through the near vacuum of space.

All waves have three characteristics: **amplitude**, **wavelength**, and **frequency**. The high points of a wave disturbance are called **crests**; the low points are called **troughs**. The amplitude of a wave is the maximum displacement from center (either the height of a crest or a trough). The wavelength of a wave is the distance from crest to crest or trough to trough and is represented by the Greek letter lambda (Λ). The frequency of a wave is the number of complete waves in a given unit of time. A frequency of one wave per second is defined as a frequency of one **hertz** (Hz).

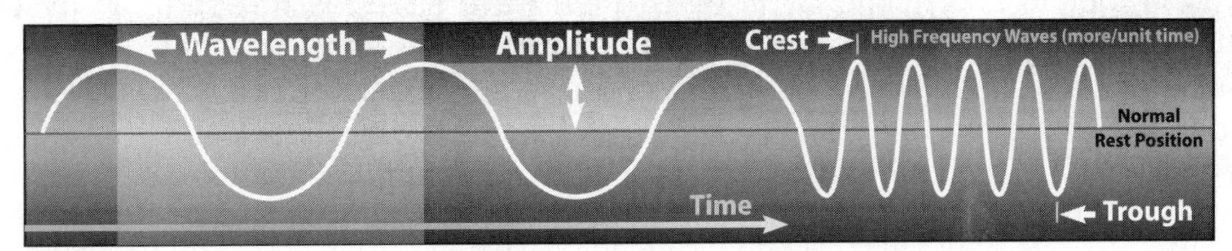

APPLY:

1. A wave is a regular disturbance that carries ______________.
2. Fernando tied a rope to a door, stretched the rope to its full length, and moved his arm up and down to create a wave. Fernando's wave is an example of a ______________ wave.
3. A wave with a frequency of 60 hertz would generate 60 wave crests every ______________.
4. X-rays, ultraviolet light, and gamma rays all can travel through interplanetary space, so they are examples of ______________ waves.
5. What happens to the amplitude of water waves as you get farther from the disturbance that caused them? ______________ Why? ______________

____

Name: ______________________________ Date: ____________________

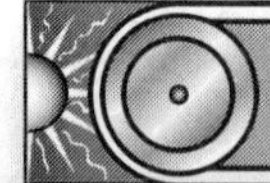

Types and Speeds of Waves

Waves can be **transverse**, **longitudinal**, or **some combination** thereof. If you "make waves" in a rope tied to a door knob, for example, the mechanical energy of the up-and-down motion of your arm is transmitted to the atoms of hemp fiber that make up the rope; they also move up and down. In **transverse waves** like these, the direction of the vibration or disturbance is perpendicular to the direction in which the wave is moving. Electromagnetic waves are also transverse; although in their case, it is the electromagnetic fields that are perpendicular to the direction of motion.

In **longitudinal waves**, the disturbed particles in the medium move in the same direction in which the wave moves. Think about the sound of a plucked guitar string. The air molecules forced away from the vibrating string bunch up when they collide with other air molecules. They become **compressed**. The area from which they move contains fewer air molecules and is **rarified**. These zones of compression and rarification continue as the wave progresses in the same direction in which the wave is moving. The crests of these waves correspond to areas of compression; troughs correspond to areas of rarification.

Surface waves in water are a kind of **combination wave** because water molecules move both up and down and forward a little, tracing out a circular path.

The **speed of a wave** equals its frequency times its wavelength. If wavelength is measured in meters and frequency in hertz, then wave speed is measured in m/sec. In a given medium (say air or water), the speed of a wave is **constant**. So, if a wave's frequency increases, the wavelength must decrease, and vice versa. The speed of a wave is also affected by the **density** of the medium (mass/volume) and its **elasticity** (how fast it can return to its original shape). Waves move more slowly in a dense medium because there is more inertia of the medium's particles to overcome. Waves also move more slowly in an inelastic medium because it requires more energy to displace the particles.

APPLY:

1. Sound travels faster in warm air than cold air. Explain. ______________________________
   ____
2. The speed of a wave equals its ____________________ x ____________________.
3. T or F? An X-ray is an example of a longitudinal wave.
4. T or F? Waves are always either transverse or longitudinal.
5. The speed of light in water should be ______________ than the speed of light in a vacuum.
6. Regions of compressed air caused by the sound of an explosion correspond to the ______________ of the sound waves.

Name: ______________________________ Date: ____________________

Wave Interactions

ABSORB:

It's fine to talk about wave properties, but waves become more interesting (like people) when we find out what they can *do* in different situations. It turns out that waves, as they travel about the universe and interact with objects and different mediums, can either experience **reflection**, **refraction**, **diffraction**, or **interference**.

A "ray" of light emitted from the sun speeds through the vacuum of space for a little over eight minutes, then whacks into the atmosphere of Earth. It slows down as it enters this denser medium. This speed change causes the light ray to bend, or **refract**. If the light ray continues and happens to enter a glass of water, its speed (and direction) will change again because water has a different density than air. This is why that pencil you stuck in your water glass looks bent. Why *did* you do that, anyway?

If the light ray had struck the shiny, "perfect attendance" button on your blouse, most of the light ray would have bounced, or **reflected**, off of it. Waves always reflect in the same way. The angle formed between an incoming ray (the **angle of incidence**) and a line perpendicular to the object (the **normal**) is always equal to the angle formed between the reflected ray (the **angle of reflection**) and that same normal. ($Angle_i = Angle_r$)

Incident Ray | Normal | Reflected | i | r | Reflecting Surface

i (angle of incidence) = r (angle of reflection)

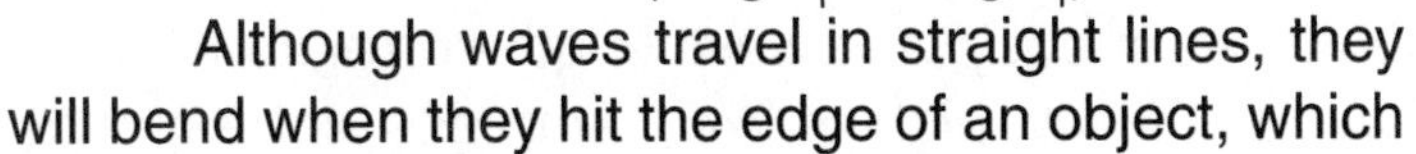

Although waves travel in straight lines, they will bend when they hit the edge of an object, which is why you can still hear your mother calling even if you are around the corner. This bending is called **diffraction**. The larger the wavelength as compared to the size of the barrier, the more the bending.

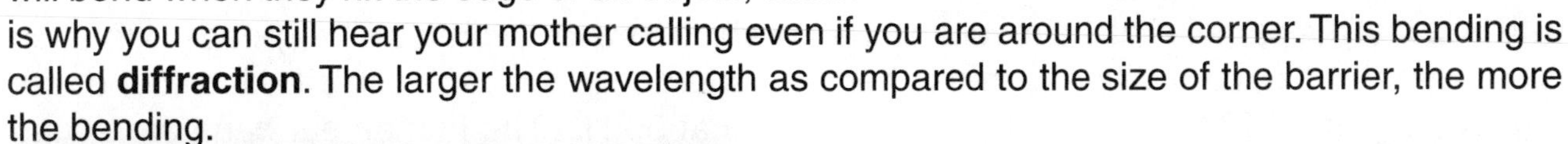

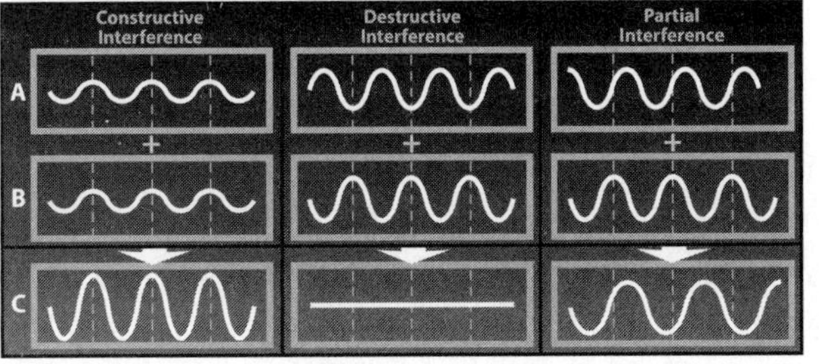

Interference results when two or more waves reach the same place at the same time. Waves **constructively interfere** with each other if their wave crests and troughs coincide. Waves **destructively interfere** with each other when the crests of one wave coincide with the troughs of another.

Sometimes waves don't appear to be moving. Such waves are called **standing waves**. The frequency of vibration for an object that produces a standing wave is called an object's **resonant frequency**. Sometimes a singer's voice will reach the same resonant frequency as a nearby glass. The glass will vibrate at that frequency, and because glass is not very flexible, it may break.

APPLY:

1. Name the type of wave interaction that is happening in the following examples:
   A. An echo: ____________________
   B. The sun is still visible even though it's slightly below horizon: ____________________
   C. Ripples of water bending around the edge of a dock: ____________________
2. If a light beam strikes a shiny object at a 90-degree angle, to what are the angle of incidence and the angle of reflection equal? ________________

Name: ______________________ Date: ______________________

Sound and Its Properties

If you vibrate matter in some way in a medium (air, water, or whatever), you have created **sound**—a wave phenomenon that our ears are designed to record. **Sound** is a longitudinal wave whose speed is dependent on the **temperature**, **elasticity**, and **density** of the medium through which it travels. Sound travels faster in solids than liquids and faster in liquids than gases because their **elasticities**—the ability of their component molecules or atoms to bounce back where they were—varies with how tightly bound those particles are to each other. That's why in those old westerns, someone would listen for the sound of approaching horses by putting his ear to the ground. Sound travels about four times faster through the earth than through the air.

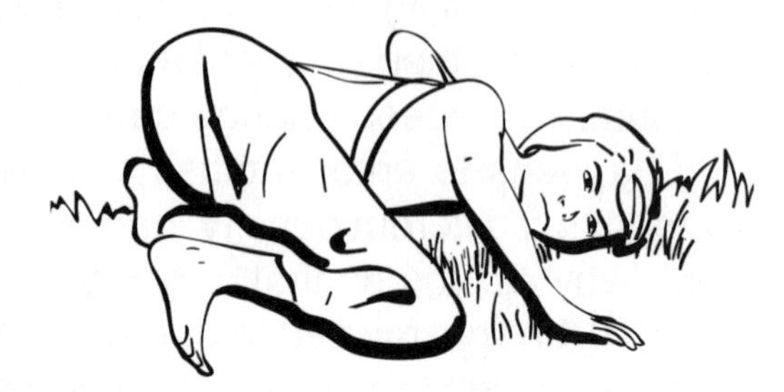

However, *in the same phase of matter*, sound will travel slower in denser material because it takes more energy to move more molecules in a given space. (There is more momentum—**mv**—there.) Sound travels faster in warm air than cold, for example. Warm air is less dense than cold air. Sound travels faster in stone than steel because stone is less dense than steel.

How do the wave properties of amplitude, frequency, and wavelength correlate with the familiar properties of sound? The **pitch** of a sound—how high or low it sounds—corresponds with how fast the particles of the medium through which it travels vibrates. The speed of vibration is the same as **frequency** (measured in hertz). A soprano in the choir can produce sound with a frequency of 1,000 Hz. Thunder produces sound at 50 Hz. The human ear can hear sound from 20–20,000 Hz—any sound greater than 20,000 Hz is **ultrasonic**. Sound that is less than 20 Hz is **infrasonic**. Cats and dogs can hear ultrasonic sounds; elephants communicate with infrasonic sounds. Aren't you jealous?

Frequency of sound also changes when the object producing that sound is moving. The frequency of sound of an approaching fire truck will increase because the sound waves moving toward the receiver (you) are being compressed (a shorter wavelength), so you hear more waves per second. As the fire truck passes, the sound waves hit your ear less often (lower frequency) because the wavelengths are longer. This wailing change in pitch is called the **Doppler effect** or the **Doppler shift**.

The **intensity** or **loudness** of sound correlates with the energy in the wave, indicated by the wave's **amplitude**. Loudness is measured in **decibels** (dB). A whisper produces 10–20 decibels, while a conversation produces 60–70 decibels. Thunder may produce 120 decibels. Anything louder than that is painful. Even music played at 85 decibels can cause ear damage.

APPLY:

1. Sound is a ______________ wave passing through some ______________.
2. The speed of sound depends on the ______________, ______________, and ______________ of the medium through which it travels.

Name: ______________________________ Date: ____________________

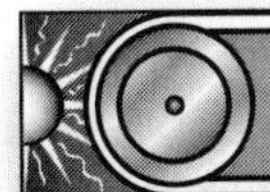

Mixing Sound Waves

ABSORB:

"And the beat goes on ..." some song lyricist said, and it certainly does. Human beings always respond to catchy beats, although the nature of those beats may vary from generation to generation. Producing and understanding high-quality, pleasing sound is the job of those who study **acoustics**, the science of sound.

Beats, by the way, are repeating changes in loudness due to sounds that are close, but not identical, in a frequency whose waves constructively interfere with each other in a regular pattern. (See page 37 to remind yourself about constructive interference.)

Musical instruments produce sound by vibrating strings, surfaces (like drum heads and cymbals), or columns of air (wind and brass instruments). The **quality** of the sound produced results from the blending of the various pitches created. Sound quality is called **timbre**. All instruments produce a **fundamental tone**, which is the lowest frequency at which that instrument can create a standing wave (see page 37). However, instruments can also produce standing waves at higher frequencies, and these are called **overtones**. The blending of the fundamental tone with these overtones produces the characteristic quality, or **timbre**, of an instrument—or an individual voice. Voice prints can capture the unique quality of output from *your* vocal cords.

Does a band produce **music** or **noise**? This is a fundamental generational question. A **sound** becomes music when it has a pleasing quality, a definite, identifiable pitch, and a repeating timing called rhythm. **Noise** has no pleasing quality, no identifiable pitch, and no definite relationship between the fundamental tone and the overtones. Ah, you now have a yardstick to compare your definition with that of your parents. The only area of contention left is the decibel level. Remember, keep it under 85 to save your hearing!

APPLY:

1. The study of sound is called ____________________.
2. T or F? Both fundamental tones and overtones represent standing waves produced by a sound source.
3. T or F? Beats in music result from the regular destructive interference of wave forms.
4. Blow across the top of a bottle, and you will hear a sound of a certain pitch. Name two ways you could change the pitch of that sound. ________________ ________________
5. Short, tight strings vibrate at a higher frequency than long, loose strings. What happens to a boy's vocal cords at puberty? ________________________________
6. Explain the difference between music and noise. ________________________________
____
7. The blending of the fundamental tone with overtones produces the ________________ of an instrument.

Name: ______________________ Date: ______________

Using Sound

ABSORB:

Animals, including bats, many whales and porpoises, and a few other mammals and birds, use sound quite effectively in a process called **echolocation**. The animals emit high frequency **ultrasound** waves that bounce off objects and moving prey. This echo tells the animal how far away obstacles and/or lunch might be. Blind humans also get quite good at "reading" echoes of nearby objects.

Humans have also perfected a device called **SONAR** (***SO***und ***N***avigation ***A***nd ***R***anging), that essentially copies the echolocation technique. This has been used in water to find old wrecks and lost cargo and to map terrain. On land, sonar can be used to look for oil, minerals, and fossils. Auto-focus cameras use sound to pinpoint the distance to the object you want to photograph.

Here's how the technique works: **distance traveled = speed x time**. Send out a sound pulse and carefully measure the time it takes to bounce back to you. Divide that number by two, and you have the time it takes for the pulse to reach the object in question. Once you know the speed of sound in the medium through which you are sending the pulse, you can calculate the distance to the object. So, if the speed of sound in water is 1,530 m/sec, and it takes 5 seconds for an echo to return from a sunken treasure ship, the ship must be 1,530 m/sec x 2.5 sec = 3,825 m below you.

Ultrasonic sound vibrations can also be used to clean jewelry, electronic components, and other delicate equipment. The objects are placed in a mild detergent of some kind, and the vibrations shake all the dirt loose.

You may also have seen the **ultrasound images** of a baby sister or cousin fastened to the refrigerator door. Ultrasound can safely image babies in the womb to make it easier to see abnormal growths and the functioning of organs so that they can be watched on video screens. High-energy varieties of ultrasound can be focused on cancers to destroy them. Ultrasounds can also produce heat for sore muscles as part of physical therapy programs.

APPLY:

1. Many animals use ______________________ to find prey.
2. A porpoise sends out an ultrasonic burst and hears the echo off his favorite food in 0.13 seconds. How far away is lunch? (Assume that sound travels at 1,530 m/sec in water.)

   ____

3. A paleontologist using ultrasound gets an echo back from a fossil in 0.10 seconds. He knows that sound travels at 5,971 m/sec in rock. How far beneath him is the fossil?

   ____

4. How would you calculate the speed of sound in a medium if you knew how far away an object was and how long it took a sound pulse to reach it through that medium?

   ____

5. Frequencies of sound waves higher than those we can hear are called ______________.

Name: ______________________________ Date: ________________

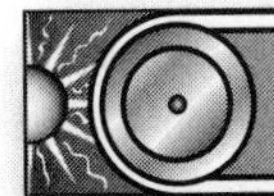

Electromagnetic Waves

ABSORB:

The electromagnetic waves we, as humans, are best equipped to sense are the waves of visible light. **Electromagnetic (em) waves** consist not of vibrating particles, but of electric and magnetic fields vibrating at right angles to each other and at right angles to the direction of the wave, or ray. As you'll recall from page 36, this makes them **transverse waves**. They need no medium through which to travel, but they do routinely pass through matter. Like other waves, they carry energy—sometimes lots of it.

The sun is the source of most of the electromagnetic radiation we encounter because the sun possesses atoms (mostly hydrogen and helium atoms) under tremendous pressures and temperatures. As we've seen, electric and magnetic fields result from moving charges. All **electromagnetic waves** come from a charge that is changing speed or direction. In the case of visible light, when negatively charged electrons gain energy, they jump farther away from the positively charged nucleus. When they lose energy and fall back, they emit a ray, or wave, of light.

As it turns out, there is a vast amount of electromagnetic energy we cannot see directly. This electromagnetic, or **em spectrum**, consists of other em waves with different **amplitudes**, **wavelengths**, and **frequencies**. All em radiation, however, travels at the same speed—the "speed of light"—which is 300 million meters per second. Because this speed is a constant, the wavelength and frequency of em waves must change together. Remember, **speed = wavelength x frequency**. Thus, long wavelengths go with low frequencies, and short wavelengths go with high frequencies. **High-frequency em waves** carry the most energy. The em spectrum extends from low-energy **radio waves** to high-energy **gamma rays**. We'll explore this expanded universe of energy shortly.

APPLY:

1. Electromagnetic waves are ________________ waves with a(n) ________________ field and a(n) ________________ field perpendicular to each other.
2. T or F? The various forms of em radiation vary in speed, amplitude, and frequency.
3. When an electron jumps from high- to low-energy levels:
   A. Radio and gamma rays are produced.
   B. A wave of visible light is produced.
   C. A wave with parallel electric and magnetic fields results.
   D. Waves of differing speeds may be produced.
4. Long wavelength radio waves have ________________ frequencies.
5. T or F? Human beings can only detect a small portion of the em spectrum with their eyes.
6. What are the physical characteristics of an em wave? ____
7. What are the ways in which sound and light are alike? What are the ways in which they are different? Answer on your own paper.

The Electromagnetic (em) Spectrum

Electromagnetic waves zip and bounce all around you! Look at the electromagnetic spectrum shown on this page as we tour em radiation from low-frequency radio waves to high-frequency gamma rays. The visible spectrum is expanded to show the colors of the rainbow (**R**ed, **O**range, **Y**ellow, **G**reen, **B**lue, **I**ndigo, and **V**iolet—**Roy G. Biv.**) Wasn't he the school counselor or something?

Radio waves are charged particles that vibrate in antennas. They are *not* the same as sound waves. Radio waves get transmitted from broadcast stations, vibrate antennas that are tuned to the proper frequency, and get converted to sound waves in radios and televisions. Radio waves can be **modulated**, or changed in **amplitude** or **frequency**. The sound portion of most TV broadcasts is **amplitude modulated** (**AM**). The picture portion is **frequency modulated** (**FM**).

Microwaves are fairly high-frequency radio waves that get water molecules vibrating and producing heat; thus, they can cook food. They agitate metal atoms so much that they can generate electric currents, which is why you keep foil out of the microwave. Microwaves can also be used for communication and weather forecasting.

Radar (***RA****dio* ***D****etecting* ***A****nd* ***R****anging*) systems use short wavelength microwaves to locate objects in a manner similar to sonar (see page 40). Police bounce microwaves off of moving vehicles with "radar guns" and calculate speed from the **Doppler effect or shift** (see page 38).

Infrared radiation: Infrared waves vibrate with a frequency just lower than visible light. We perceive these waves as heat. With the special lenses of night-vision goggles, you can see the infrared radiation given off by living things. About 50 percent of the radiation given off by the sun is in the infrared range.

Visible light: More on this shortly. It is critical for life functions like **photosynthesis**.

Ultraviolet (UV) radiation: These have slightly higher frequencies than visible light. Various insects and other arthropods can see these frequencies. Certain minerals give off light when exposed to UV light. UV light causes sunburn. Living things are partly shielded from UV light by the **ozone layer**—molecules of triple-bonded oxygen in the upper atmosphere.

X-rays are produced by the decay of certain radioactive materials and in the explosions of stars. They can pass through skin and muscle, but are stopped by bone, which is why they are used to make X-ray images. In large doses, they cause tissue damage, including various cancers like leukemia.

Gamma rays are also emitted by radioactive substances and in stellar explosions. They can pierce 3-meter-thick blocks of concrete.

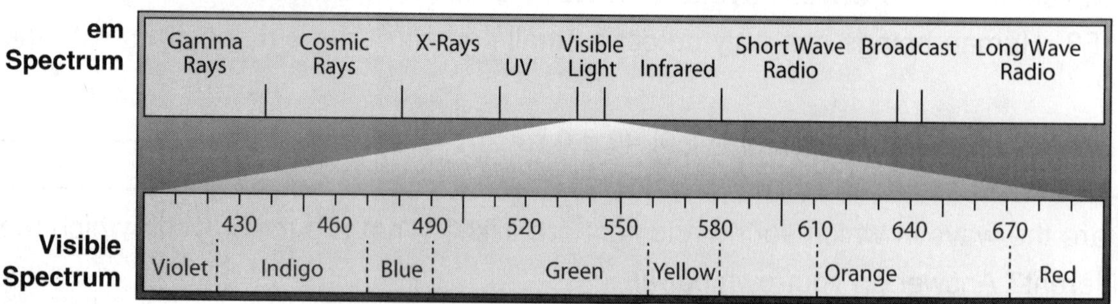

Name: ______________________________ Date: ____________________

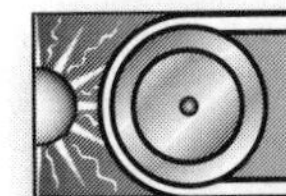

Visible Light: A "Wavicle"

ABSORB:

Luminous objects, like the sun, fireflies, and matches, give off their own visible light. That light then bounces, or reflects, off various objects, turning them into **illuminated objects**—like the moon, Ming the firefly catcher, or a cigarette smoker. Luminous objects can give off three kinds of light: **incandescent light**, **fluorescent light**, or **neon light**.

Heat sources, like the sun and a match, produce incandescent light. Incandescent light bulbs emit light when thin, tungsten filaments get their atoms all excited and heat up as electric currents flow through them. Friction ignites the phosphorous on the end of a match.

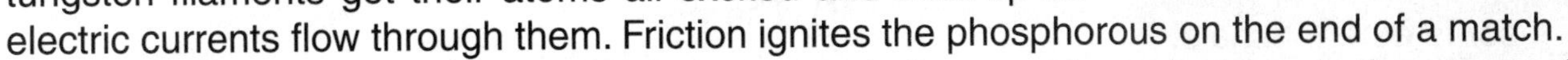

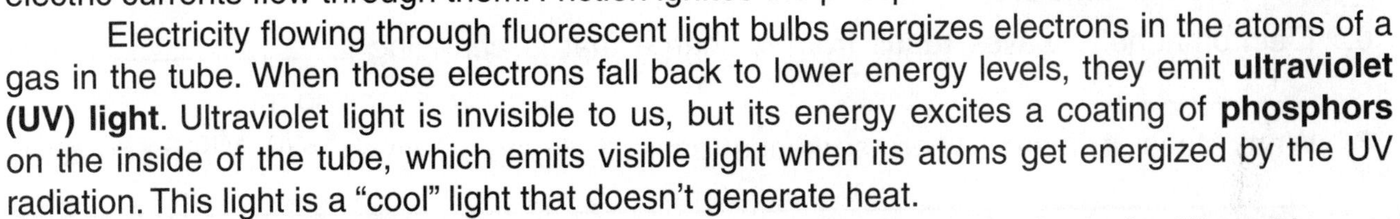

Electricity flowing through fluorescent light bulbs energizes electrons in the atoms of a gas in the tube. When those electrons fall back to lower energy levels, they emit **ultraviolet (UV) light**. Ultraviolet light is invisible to us, but its energy excites a coating of **phosphors** on the inside of the tube, which emits visible light when its atoms get energized by the UV radiation. This light is a "cool" light that doesn't generate heat.

Another cool light is neon light, generated by electricity flowing in a tube filled with neon gas. Neon gas emits red light. Mercury vapor lights emit greenish-blue light, and sodium vapor lamps emit yellow-orange light.

Light, as we've seen, has many wave-like properties. It's transmitted by oscillating electric and magnetic fields. When light passes through two narrow slits, it forms an interference pattern on paper or photographic film that looks just like the pattern formed by intersecting waves. But, around the turn of the century, **Albert Einstein** and other scientists showed that light has particle-like characteristics, too.

Shine red light—no matter how bright—on a certain kind of metal plate, and nothing happens. Shine violet light—no matter how weak—on that same plate, and electrons get knocked around and begin to flow. Light behaves as if it were striking the plate, in tiny particles (called **photons** or **quanta** by scientists). Red light just can't deliver enough energy to the plate, no matter how intense it is, but violet light can. This phenomenon is called the **photoelectric effect** and is the basis for such devices as "electric eyes," certain light meters, and video sound tracks.

Look at the em spectrum on page 42. Violet light has a higher frequency (and shorter wavelength) than red light. The **energy of photons (or quanta of any em radiation)** is proportional to its frequency. As difficult as it is to wrap our brains around the idea, visible light and other em radiation travel like waves, but hit detectors like mini-bullets of energy.

APPLY:

Describe light's wave-like and particle-like properties. ______________________________

____

____

Name: ______________________ Date: ______________

Part 5: Waves of Light and Sound: Putting It All Together

CONTENT REVIEW

1. Waves can carry either ______________ or ______________ energy.
2. A compression wave, like sound, is a kind of ______________ wave.
3. When a wave reflects off of a surface, the angle of ______________ always equals the angle of ______________.
4. The wailing change of pitch you hear as a locomotive approaches and then recedes from you is called the __________ __________.
5. T or F? Ultrasonic cleaners are based on the same principle as echolocation in bats and some other animals.
6. Electromagnetic waves result from a charge that is changing ______________ or ______________.
7. What does it mean when someone says that radio waves can be modulated? ______________________________
8. The photoelectric effect shows that light can behave like a(n) ______________.
9. ______________ light is produced by heat.
10. The timbre of a sound is a measure of its ______________.
11. All em radiation travels at what speed? ______________

CONCEPT REVIEW

1. Scientists once thought that outer space was filled with a thin substance called ether in order to explain how light travels. Why might they have thought that was so? ______________________________
2. Why does the amount of sound in a room decrease after putting carpeting and furniture in it? ______________________________
3. The Doppler effect or shift can be observed with light just as with sound. The frequency of light emitted from a star shifts, depending on whether it is moving toward or away from Earth. Would a yellow star's color become redder or bluer if it were moving away from Earth? Explain. ______________________________
4. Some people have observed that animal behavior changes just before an earthquake. What might explain this? ______________________________
5. "An oven cooks from the outside in, and a microwave cooks from the inside out." Explain why this is a true statement. ______________________________

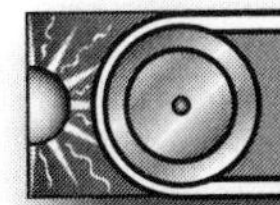

Answer Keys

A Universe of Motion, Forces, and Energy (Page 2)
1. frame of reference; 2. metric; 3. motion, forces, energy (any order); 4. 4,545.5 kg; 5. earth

Part 1: Measuring Tools: Measuring With Metrics (Page 4)
1. Variable answers; 2. Variable answers; 3. 51.5; 4. 34; 5. 6 million; 6. A. 120; B. 127; C. 914.4; D. 1,000; E. 3,048

Part 2: The Mechanics of Motion: Measuring Speed and Velocity (Page 6) 1. 96; 59.7; 2. 12; 3. 1.67 m/min, 1.5 m/min; 4. A. Speed; B. Velocity; C. Velocity; D. Speed; 5. Vector will be 1.75 cm long (350 km), pointing north.

Get Ready, Get Set, Accelerate! (Page 7) 1. 45 m, 108 m, 15 m/sec, 24 m/sec, 3 m/sec/sec; 2. 8.75 km/sec/sec; 3. No, Yes. Earth is rotating and revolving around the sun. 4. D.

Conserving Mother Mo(mentum) (Page 8) 1. 7 kg-m/sec; 2. Taxi, because it weighs so much more than a baseball. 3. 4.5 m/sec; 4. mass, velocity (any order); 5. Run faster. 6. Space shuttle, freight train, Volkswagen, bullet, fly; 7. Most of it is transferred to the pins.

A Feeling for Forces (Page 9) 1. push or pull; 2. F; 3. Vector 4 centimeters long pointing right; 4. A. Sliding, B. Fluid, C. Rolling

Newton's Big 3 (Page 10) 1. 4,500 N; 2. The wrestler; 3. The force of its wingbeat against air propels the bird forward.

Free Fa-a-all and Gravity (Page 11) 1. 29.4 m/sec; 2. It decreases rapidly because force decreases by the inverse square of the distance between objects. 3. Weight will decrease; mass will stay the same.

Forces in Fluids (Page 12) 1. The ship's overall density (including the density of the air-filled hull) is less than the density of an equal volume of water. 2. Air masses flow from areas of high pressure to areas of low pressure, producing wind.

Work and Power (Page 13) 1. joules; watts; 2. Variable; 3. Divide work by 10; divide work by 4; 4. A and C are work; 5. 1,000,000 watts; 6. F

Part 2: The Mechanics of Motion: Putting It All Together (Page 15)
<u>**CONTENT**</u>: 1. distance, time, direction; 2. T; 3. The total momentum (mv) of a group of objects remains the same, although it may be transferred among objects in the group; 4. vectors; 5. F = ma; 6. A. 7. Bernoulli's; 8. W = Fd, P = W/time or work equals force used to move an object; power equals how fast work happens; 9. simple machines
<u>**CONCEPT**</u>: 1. Several different wedges; 2. The force used to move the groceries is perpendicular to the groceries; 3. The time it took. 4. The second person's average speed was greater than the first person's constant speed; 5. It takes a while to slow the momentum of large objects; 6. Gravity, air movements; 7. Answers will vary.

Part 3: All About Energy: Energy, Let Me Count Its Forms (Page 16) 1. A. Chemical energy; B. Nuclear energy; C. Electromagnetic energy; D. Heat energy; E. Mechanical energy; 2. sun; 3. the ability to do work

Kinetic Energy: The Energy of Motion (Page 17) 1. Kinetic energy increases with the square of velocity; 2. work; 3. 22,500 J; 4. Momentum = mv and has direction; K.E. = $mv^2/2$ and is not a vector; 5. potential, kinetic (any order); 6. F

Potential Energy: The Energy of Position (Page 18)
1. position; 2. F; 3. 2,058,750 J; 4. 6,669,000 J; 5. B.; 6. height and weight (any order)

Energy Conversions (Page 19) 1. chemical, heat, mechanical; 2. energy conversions; 3. Mechanical energy of water, mechanical energy of moving turbines, electric energy, mechanical energy of dryer fan, heat energy of dryer coils. 4. At release; when it hits the ground and when it stops rolling; just before the first bounce; 5. A. solar cells; B. burning fossil fuel, a match, etc.; C. friction

Moving Heat Around: Thermodynamics (Page 20)
1. No convection or conduction of heat through the vacuum; no heat loss by radiation through the shiny liner. 2. There is some loss by conduction through the stopper and lid.

Conserve Energy—That's the Law! (Page 21) 1. F; 2. Fossil fuels; heat, mechanical, electromagnetic; 3. Under very high temperatures and pressures, mass can be converted to energy; 4. heat

The Laws of Thermodynamics (Page 22) 1. 600 J; 2. First Law; 3. There are always some heat losses in any machine.

Entropy: A Measure of Disorder (Page 23) 1. heat; 2. Somewhat disordered and chaotic; 3. Eventually, the universe will all be at the same temperature, and there will be no energy to do work. 4. When there is a concentrated source of energy, like the sun. 5. Light and other em radiation, electricity, fossil fuels; 6. C.

Part 3: All About Energy: Putting It All Together (Page 24)
<u>**CONTENT**</u>: 1. joules; 2. C.; 3. kinetic; 4. weight; 5. heat and light; 6. conduction, convection, radiation (any order); 7. Energy can neither be created nor destroyed by ordinary means. 8. the First Law of Thermodynamics; 9. F
<u>**CONCEPT**</u>: 1. Heat from radioactive elements increases with depth; 2. Potential energy; 3. Sir Seymour; his cannonballs will

have more kinetic energy because velocity is more important than mass in increasing kinetic energy. 4. Jupiter; 5. T; 6. In order for objects to be cooled, energy must be expended. Heat is the byproduct.

Part 4: Electricity and Magnetism: Force, Charge, and Atomic Structure (Page 25) 1. +2; 2. It will bend the stream flow by attracting the positive end of the water molecules.

Electric Forces and Fields (Page 26) 1. F; 2. T; 3. Electric potential is the amount of electrical potential energy per amount of charge. Electrical potential energy is charge not performing work. 4. toward; 5. potential

Magnets and Magnetic Induction (Page 27) 1. A.; 2. attract; 3. monopoles

Magnetic Fields (Page 28) 1. magnetic fields; 2. Their magnetic domains become randomly oriented.; 3. Iron, nickel, cobalt; 4. north, south; 5. A.; 6. atoms, field lines

Forces, Electric Currents, and Magnetic Fields (Page 29) 1. C.; 2. F; 3. magnetic moments.

Linking Moving Charges and Changing Magnetic Fields (Page 30) 1. electric current; 2. galvanometers; 3. change the direction of current flow so the armature keeps spinning. 4. F; 5. The compass is attracted or repelled by the magnetic field of the current.

EMFs and Circuits (Page 31) 1. 12-volt battery;
2. electromotive; 3. Complete circuit and device connected to circuit; 4. positive;
5.

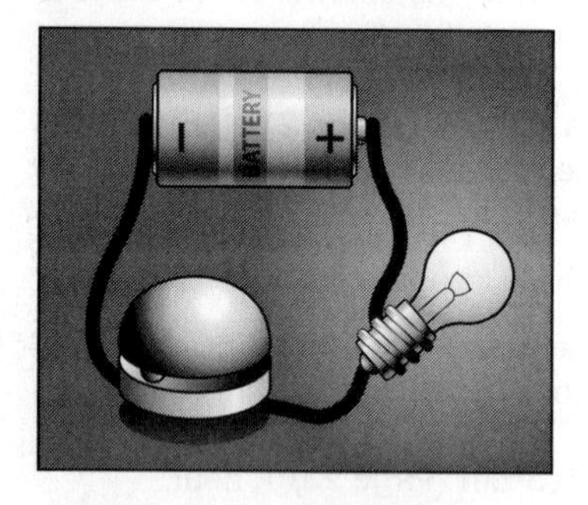

Ohm's Law and Resistance (Page 32) 1. electrons; 2. F; 3. 5 amps; 4. 0.15 ohms

Power Production and Transformers (Page 33) 1. F; 2. Step-up transformer increases output voltage; step-down transformer decreases output voltage. 3. B.; 4. mechanical; 5. F

Part 4: Electricity and Magnetism: Putting It All Together (Page 34)
CONTENT: 1. positive, neutral, negative; 2. positive, negative; 3. F; 4. Groups of atoms of a substance that align themselves with a magnetic field; 5. T; 6. current; 7. circuit; 8. V = IR, amps, volts; 9. It will have fewer.
CONCEPT: 1. Forces are both inversely proportional to the distance between objects, but constants are very different in size. 2. An electric charge was induced in the hairs, and they lined up with the electric field lines; 3. The magnetic domains got randomized; 4. The currents in the wires were moving in the same direction, creating magnetic fields with the same polarity. 5. Series. More current is available to flow through the remaining lights because there is one less resistor in the circuit.

Part 5: Waves of Light and Sound: Waves and Their Properties (Page 35) 1. energy; 2. mechanical; 3. second; 4. electromagnetic; 5. It decreases, because energy is continually lost.

Types and Speeds of Waves (Page 36) 1. Warm air is less dense, so particles get disturbed more easily. 2. frequency x wavelength; 3. F; 4. F; 5. slower; 6. crests

Wave Interactions (Page 37) 1. A. Reflection, B. Refraction, C. Diffraction; 2. 0°

Sound and Its Properties (Page 38) 1. longitudinal, medium; 2. density, temperature, elasticity (any order)

Mixing Sound Waves (Page 39) 1. acoustics; 2. T; 3. F; 4. Add water to the bottle; blow across the top at a different speed; 5. They get longer and looser; 6. Music has a pleasing quality and a definite pitch and rhythm; noise doesn't; 7. timbre

Using Sound (Page 40) 1. echolocation; 2. 99.45 m; 3. 298.55 m; 4. Speed = distance/time 5. ultrasonic

Electromagnetic Waves (Page 41) 1. transverse, electric, magnetic (last two in any order); 2. F; 3. B.; 4. low; 5. T;
6. amplitude, wavelength, and frequency; 7. Both have wave properties; light is an em transverse wave; sound is a longitudinal, mechanical wave.

Visible Light: A "Wavicle" (Page 43) Light vibrates as it travels and creates interference patterns like a wave, but it delivers energy on impact in discrete, particle-like photons.

Part 5: Waves of Light and Sound: Putting It All Together (Page 44)
CONTENT: 1. mechanical, electromagnetic (any order); 2. longitudinal; 3. incidence, reflection; 4. Doppler effect (or shift); 5. F; 6. speed or direction (any order); 7. The frequencies or amplitudes of the waves can be changed. 8. particle;
9. Incandescent; 10. quality; 11. The speed of light (300 million meters/sec)
CONCEPT: 1. Other waves require a medium in which to propagate.; 2. Sound is absorbed and scattered by carpet and irregular surfaces.; 3. Redder. Frequencies of light would decrease.; 4. Animals may perceive sound or other vibrations that people can't.; 5. Microwave energy vibrates water molecules throughout the food; heat transfers from oven coils by convection and conduction.